赢在北美
Win in North America

——青少年北美留学必备

郑璨 著

中央广播电视大学出版社 · 北京

图书在版编目（CIP）数据

赢在北美：青少年北美留学必备：汉英对照／郑璨著. -- 北京：中央广播电视大学出版社，2016.1

ISBN 978 - 7 - 304 - 07585 - 9

Ⅰ. ①赢… Ⅱ. ①郑… Ⅲ. ①留学生教育—概况—北美洲—汉语、英语 Ⅳ. ①G649.71

中国版本图书馆 CIP 数据核字（2015）第 307337 号

赢在北美——青少年北美留学必备
YING ZAI BEIMEI——QINGSHAONIAN BEIMEI LIUXUE BIBEI
郑　璨　著

出版·发行　中央广播电视大学出版社
电话：营销中心 010 - 66490011　　　总编室 010 - 68182524
网址：http://www.crtvup.com.cn
地址：北京市海淀区西四环中路 45 号　**邮编：**100039
经销：新华书店北京发行所

策划编辑：张　暾　　　　　　　　**版式设计：**何智杰
责任编辑：刘桂伟　　　　　　　　**责任校对：**赵　洋
责任印制：赵连生

印刷：北京宏伟双华印刷有限公司
版本：2016 年 1 月第 1 版　　　　2016 年 1 月第 1 次印刷
开本：130mm×187mm　　　　　**印张：**5.375　**字数：**87 千字

书号： ISBN 978 - 7 - 304 - 07585 - 9
定价：28.90 元

作者简介

郑璨，获得加拿大维多利亚大学英语硕士学位，主修现代主义文学。《全球文论：文选》（*Global Literary Theory：An Anthology*）贡献者之一。

主要作品

Out of the Cocoon，Are You the Butterfly?
The Nest—Poems 2014
Sage

致我的父母

序

　　此书适用于在北美高中就读，以及刚刚进入北美大学的中国学生。尤其适用于十二年级处于大学准备阶段，渴望深入认识自我、明确未来方向、实现梦想的中国青少年。

　　在全球化的浪潮里，各民族文化高度融合，中国青少年流散在世界各地也已经成为一大现象。少年时代出国读书的中国孩子，不管有没有家长陪读，不管在国内上过多久的国际学校，都会或多或少地在真正的英语环境中面临一些困难。更有些学生在国外读私立高中4年、大学本科8年、硕士4年还是迟迟不能毕业。即使在公立高中数理成绩全A的同学，英语语文素养、批判性思维能力、英语写作能力仍然是让他们最头疼的，但这些能力是进入大学以前需要掌握的基本功。在多伦多教英语写作和英语文学期间，我接触到从八年级到初进大一的学生，所有学生都面临共同的困惑——如何在中、西两种文化的夹缝之间寻找和确立自我身份？这些问题在本书前两部分"成长篇"和"成就篇"中会总结并涉及。而第三部分"实践篇"介绍了所有准备在北美读大学的学生必备的基本学习技能。

当前，北美文化的核心也是其教育环境中文化的核心，它重视"自我实现"式的成功和在后殖民文化中的自我定位，强调个人对世界的贡献等。"成长篇"以最浅显的方式，带领青少年读者深入北美文化，了解并找到真正的自己以及自己和世界的关系。在教学中，我发现，本书前两篇总结的相关知识能从根源上解决中国学生在北美所遇到的各种困难，这是仅仅通过学习写作或学习英语小说、戏剧、诗歌难以实现的，而学生们都迫切需要这些知识，因为我已经看到他们每个人的转变。

此书绝不推崇英汉互译的英语教育理念（始终处于自我翻译状态的大脑是不可能把英语学地道的），作者鼓励青少年读者直接阅读英文部分——因为你们已经具备了这个阅读能力。来北美学习的同学应该尽早放弃大脑中英汉互译的习惯，学会要么直接用中文思考，要么直接用英文思考，否则无法快速提高英语水平。中文部分的文字并不是对英文部分文本的严格翻译，它与英文部分的文本并非一一对应的关系，这也是为了强迫读者分别阅读本书的中文部分和英文部分。

不管身处世界的哪个角落，都要记住：你不是渺小的，你的潜力是无限的，你的自信是无条件的，你的根基是强大的。我相信每个中国孩子都能在世界上找到自己的位置，每个中国孩子都能让世界为你而喝彩。

郑璨

2015 年 10 月

多伦多

目 录 *Contents*

实践篇　自我训练

成长篇

自我发现

第一讲　文化转换

　　到英语国家进入公立或私立中学、大学的中国学生都会经历一个必然的文化转换过程。在北美"自我实现"的文化环境中，如果没有明确自己的个性和人生目标，你将很难成为佼佼者。北美的中小学教育会深入引导你"发现"（大学教育帮助"实现"）自己的人生使命，因为这是一个孩子各种潜能自然爆发的关键。"潜能"是自我的无限状态——它几乎超越了当下你对自己的所有认识。发掘自己的各种未知潜力看上去是个恐怖而庞杂的工程，但通过带你寻求自我的根基，我将使此旅程最简化。

　　大部分年纪较小的中国学生来到北美是为了求学。当英语成为第二语言，当你开始接触北美的教育系统，你也开始在文化身份转换的轨道上坐起过山车。在北美学校已经上了一两年学的同学，肯定已经有了这种文化身份转换的感受，但可能还不知道该如何解决这个问题。也许，你有时会感觉自己像钟摆一样，在中、西方文化之间摆动，这种困惑会持续一段时间，但它也会滋养你，让你成长，直到有一天你能建立起一个源于中国文化的新的自我。

所谓个性

中国有几千年的悠久历史和灿烂文化，相比之下，北美历史和文化显得太过"年轻"，但这并不意味着两种文化孰优孰劣——它们只是不同，有各自的优点。比如，博大精深的中国文化蕴含着许多经过时间检验的智慧，而北美文化则善于汲取全世界各种文化中的"真理"，善于创造新的文化体系。

中国文化注重民族的凝聚力，即集体的力量，大家需要共同协作，集体的强大也是个人的强大。群体之间的互相依赖与合作非常重要，从传统上讲，这有可能使一个人在独处时感到不自在或没有安全感，这是大部分中国学生出国生活面临的第一挑战，即你如何接受和适应自我的独立存在感。

尽管过去几十年间，全球化促使世界上的各种文化极速碰撞，彼此融合，北美文化中的集体性观念越来越强，但在整个西方，个人主义仍然是有着千年历史的、成熟的传统。在后殖民主义之后的最前沿的北美文化中，个人主义有着向东方文化学习的趋势，甚至近几年，北美比以往更强调集体（community）的概念，因为个人主义在过去一个世纪的西方历史上经受众多磨难以后，已经清楚地意识到：个人的价值必须通过惠及他人来实现。

但从传统上来说，个人主义强调自我，强调个性，强调自我与他人的区别。在北美的中国学生既需要了解西方文化的根基，也需要了解北美文化的前进方向。

很多中国学生一到北美就感受到这一点，亚洲学生扎堆就是一大体现。举个简单的例子，一些同学哪怕在成年以后，独处也会觉得没有安全感，上学得有人陪，吃饭、购物也得有人陪，否则会感觉不自在。越抗拒改变，依赖性就越难以克服。能迈出独立的第一步，就是新的成长。变化并不意味着你忘了自己是中国人或违背自己，而是说，在北美文化身份自由选择的环境下，尽早建立成熟独立的自我体系是每个孩子无法逃避的过程。建立个性的第一步是要成为独立思考、独立行动的个体。

独一无二

很多同学在小时候个性受到压抑，长大后这些被压抑的部分可能仍会影响着他们对自我的认识。也许在你小时候，父母、老师教育你不要太"奇葩"，不要太"鹤立鸡群"。也许你经常听到这样的话："不要做那个第一个发言的""等到别人说完后你再说……"鹤立鸡群的人也许会面临太多非议，也许会受到孤立。相反，有些家长想方设法让孩子个性出众，想让他们走到哪里都光彩照人，但是孩子只是想默默无闻地做自己。个性在于你知道自己为什么是独一无二的，并"完全接受"自己的方方面面，而不是按照别人的模样去塑造自己，也不是按照别人的期待去改变自己。

世界上没有第二个你，也没有第二个人能替代你在这个世界上的位置。一个真正强大的个体在于认清自我的与众不同，并能用它服务他人。北美文化极其强调个人的选择。不论你有多"普通"，都应该不同于任何人。发掘自己独一无二的地方可以帮你意识到你的潜力在何处，也可以帮助你在学业成功上奠定重要的基础。这样你就不会人云亦云，不会在任何时候拿自己跟别人比，不会在任何时候觉得自己不如他人，不会在任何时候违背自己。有句话说："做真实的自己，然后世界会因你而改变。"

有声性

沉默无声并不是一个消极词，正相反，它有独特的价值。大部分中国学生都会面临北美学校的老师或同学的指责，说他们不说话，不发言，上课不积极参与讨论。事实上，大部分中国孩子都是课下问题很多，课上从来不敢举手打断老师提问，或者不敢当着其他同学的面问问题。他们都很乖，害怕说错或出丑。关于这一点，我们必须知道一个基本常识，那就是，西方传统的文化特点之一是逻各斯中心主义，或语言中心主义，它把"不说话"等同于"没思想"。西方哲学、文艺理论前沿已经对此特点进行了质疑和解构，但并没有根除它。大部分情况下，学校仍然要求学生用语言表达自己，这意味着学生必须学会发言，练就演讲能力，学会在各种场合发出自己独一无二的声音。

根据我的经验，中国学生通常不善发言有如下几个原因：第一，学生知道答案，但觉得不需要说出来。第二，学生知道答案，但希望别人能先说出来。第三，学生知道答案，但不是在以语言的形式思考，知识是潜在的，学生不知道如何把思想变成话语。第三种情况也是造成学生写作困难的主要原因。并不了解这一点的老师，有可能会轻易地给学生下定论，认为学生逻辑思维能力和批判性思维能力差，有语言障碍，或者干脆说这些学生"没法教"。这给高中生学习英语写作和高中英语语文（如 ENG3U/4U）带来很大打击。"不出声"并不等于智力有缺陷（整个北美都在流行瑜伽和冥想，来训练大脑关闭"语言"，以此达到"无声"的境界）。"不出声"的形象思维有它的价值，语言中心主义的线性思维也有它的价值，但是后者更容易掌握。经过一段时间的训练，学生的逻辑思维能力是可以培养起来的。

逻辑性

学会"如何思考"是整个北美中学、大学教育的终极目标，是让学生终身受用的能力，也是为什么北美高等教育领先于世界的原因。从中国最早的文字——甲骨文可以看出，中文是通过对自然的模仿而创立的，注重想象力和感知力。而英文，如瑞士语言学家费尔迪南·德·索绪尔（Ferdinand de Saussure）所说，是具有"任意性"的符号系统，也就是说，文字的形式与意义无关，它强调语法、规范、逻辑的完整性和严谨性。英语的书面语和口语必须严格符合语法，否则难以理解。这就是为什么当中国学生开始用英语交流、写作时，语法（如时态）会成为让他们头疼的问题。中国学生也有长处，比如，学习英语小说、戏剧他们觉得很吃力，但是英语诗歌往往是他们的强项，这可能得益于中文天生的图像性。母语是英语的人也会犯语法错误，但从认知上讲，这是不同于中国学生的另一种错误。中国学生常犯的语法错误诸如：句子结构不完整，语篇逻辑模糊，重复讲一个意思，等等。这是因为，中国学生往往反复描述的是图像，而不是以语法形式存在的抽象思维。

逻辑思维能力是学习的工具，你要有意识地花时间去培养，要学会区分大脑的汉语思维模式和英语思维模式，并让它们各自积极地发挥作用。在本书的"实践篇"中，我会给出一些简单易学的逻辑思维训练，这些训练会教你在英语写作中，特别是在十一、十二年级以后的学术写作中，打开思维的结，把形象思维变成线性逻辑思维。在北美上高中的中国学生最头疼的部分可能是十一、十二年级的英语，以及大学本科水平以上的学术写作。写作能力、逻辑思维能力是基本功，需要经过长期的训练，但无论如何，你应该在上大学之前具备写作能力和逻辑思维能力，这样你才能在忙碌的大学生活中把时间花在拓展专业能力上。

第二讲　发现天赋

　　在北美，自我会在各种情况下经历一次或几次转变。如果个性没有强大和相对稳定的根基，这些转变很可能扰乱自我体系，让你有时候觉得不知道自己是谁。建立个性的关键是弄清你的天赋所在。世界上不可能有第二个你，哪怕是亲兄弟姐妹，也不可能拥有你所拥有的天赋。比如，你是音乐天才，但世界上也有很多音乐神童，你跟别人相比有什么不同吗？美国作家迪帕克·乔普拉（Deepak Chopra）在《成功的 7 大精神法则》（*The Seven Spiritual Laws of Success*）第 9 章中提到，即使你同他人有相似的天赋，但"表达"此天赋的方式一定与众不同。我认为，"天赋"是上天赐予的能力，从某种程度上说，它不大需要后天学习，而后天的学习可以正向或负向地刺激该天赋发挥到极致。"不大需要学习"还说明，正因为你拥有该天赋，才应该由你从某种程度上来教育这个世界——否则上天为何赐予你这些天赋？你的天赋和你使用它的方式，基本上可以定义你为什么是独一无二的。

　　以前曾有家长问我，他们为什么总找不到自己孩子的天赋——觉得自己的孩子实在是太普通了！其实，天赋不一定是光鲜的，不是每个人都是嘎嘎小姐（Lady Gaga）或者斯蒂芬·霍金（Stephen Hawking），但每个人都有天赋。比如，有些学生很有条理，很善于整理房间，他们可能以后有出色的管理能力；有些孩子不爱受约束，让他们遵守规矩很难，他们以后可能是杰出的领导者，能轻松胜任 CEO、老板、导演等角色。家长、学生都应该意识到的一点是，所谓的天赋，可以是重大的，也可以是看上去"微不足道"的，但是每个人的天赋都是珍贵的，没有人比别人高一等或矮一截，因为人类的进步需要每个人的天赋，需要每个人的贡献。

品酌痛苦

天赋，作为某种宝藏，有可能被埋藏在你的创伤里。换句话说，人们之所以有某种独特的天赋，往往是因为他们有某种特定的痛苦。在茫然的情况下，发现天赋的第一个简单的方法是品酌你所经受的困难。也许你的人生至此一帆风顺、毫无烦恼——那么祝贺你，你可以直接跳到下一节。这一节适合那些将自己的天赋埋藏较深、在青少年时期感到压抑的学生阅读。他们或多或少因为世界看不到他们的闪光点而感到有点痛苦，或者相当痛苦。

有一个规律是，在你成为真正的自己之前，往往首先是自己的反面。有个典型的例子：我辅导过的一个华裔学生在递交申请两小时后就收到了滑铁卢大学有条件录取的电子邮件。这个学生很喜欢旅行，梦想探索世界，并能把自己的爱好和梦想与学习、工作结合起来。我在辅导她时，发现她周游世界的梦想被家庭环境所压抑，压抑到多深她自己也不太清楚，她自己也不知道自己到底为什么喜欢地理与环境管理专业，直到聊了很多故事以后，我才弄明白她对地理与环境的交叉学科如此感兴趣的原因。虽然她家在多伦多很多年，但正如大多数的中国家庭一样，父母不希望她离家到处旅行，责任和义务使得她必须要放弃很多梦想。但正因为如此，她被压抑的欲望越来越成为她自己明确的目标。所有的"痛苦"都有其存在的原因，它的价值在于帮助你认清你到底想要什么。

你想做什么说明你擅长做什么，这是生命与你对话、让你发现自己的天赋所在的特有方式。比如，一个学生想成为大明星，但她很抑郁，因为父母让她往其他方向发展，可能因此她很难绽放自己的光芒。还有一个学生有非常强的同理心，具有人道主义精神，但他生活的外部环境使他不得不以利己的方式存在。这个男孩变得内向，不爱说话，只有在别人真正理解和认可他的人道主义内心时，他才开始自信。这些事例说明，你的最深层面的痛苦指向的是你真正的愿望，而这些愿望同时暗示你擅长做什么。因此，在我们的成长过程中，应该好好利用那些影响你心灵最深的事情，找到天赋所在，找到向往所在。

聆听心声

另一种情形是，有些学生太多才多艺，他们擅长做很多事情，他们有太多的兴趣爱好，以至于他们很难发现"到底什么是我真正擅长做的"，或者"我到底想要什么"。认识自己是一个历程，你得花点时间去耐心地、充分地探索自己的方方面面，然后给自己的所有优势排一个序，从而让你把有限的精力放在最重要的事情上。

这里给你发现自己天赋的第二个策略，就是学会聆听那些反复出现的直觉，学会辨别哪些是自己内心真实的声音。有些学生很辛苦，要上很多课程，如音乐课、绘画课、舞蹈课等，同时还要做志愿者。如果你感觉很累或者有太多的所谓天赋要发展，那么，你应该知道，有些内心的愿望是真实的，而有些可能来自于虚荣心，也就是说，我们可能因为别人而做出一些决定，而忽视自己人生真正的方向。我小时候很迷恋钢琴，可我弹了几年后发现，自己并不擅长这个乐器。我又很喜欢阅读、电影、创作，在不同的兴趣爱好之间徘徊会分散很多精力。表面上看，我很茫然，但其实我在内心有非常清楚的答案。内心的真实声音有个特点，那就是，它始终存在，如果你背叛这个声音，它会越来越响。经过时间的检验，你应该相信自己内心声音的真实性，应该顺从自己的内心，因为它会把你带到正确的方向上。

当你学会倾听自己的心声、尊重自己内心感受的时候，你会发现，有些天赋是一定排在第一位的，你会自然而然地花更多时间和精力去发展它。对于多才多艺的青少年来说，你需要给自己擅长的事情排个序，放弃该放弃的，这样才能早日踏上自我实现的道路。

快乐原则

如果使用以上两个策略，你还是无法发现自己的天赋，或者你深信自己只是个普普通通的人，那么，快乐原则会帮你锁定你的天赋到底在哪里。在北美，任何成功教练都讲求快乐原则的作用，这已经成为常识。英文中有太多词可以表示"快乐"，在我看来，joy 一词表示一种深层次的喜悦感和满足感，或者说，指你在做某件让你着迷的事情时的心理状态。当你做一件事情时，你可以自然而然地全身心投入其中，废寝忘食，不觉得自己在"努力"，不觉得自己在受"累"，外界干扰也很难让你分心。找到这种快乐，也能帮你找到自己擅长的领域。

让快乐引导自己和让兴趣引导自己是不一样的，后者可能是误导。特别是在青少年时代，人格还在发展过程中，所谓的"兴趣"很可能来自旁人（喜欢的明星、朋友、社区环境等）的影响。比如，你喜欢摇滚乐，但你发现自己组建的乐队到后来不了了之。再比如，你想学习拍电影，花很多时间在这件事上，全是因为受朋友的影响。事后你可能发现，自己并不想成为导演，而只是潜意识里怕跟朋友们玩不到一起而已。这些都不是真实的自己，也不是所谓的天赋。

真正使用快乐原则的人不会感到无聊或者受限制，而会感到自我被拓展，潜力向无限发展，不知不觉在努力却感觉不到辛苦。比如，有些学生喜欢西方哲学，他们很善于拓展自己的大脑，对他们而言，在学习时，两个小时就像二十分钟。再比如，有些学生喜欢在聚光灯下的感觉，深知舞台就是自己的天堂。还有些学生喜欢与人交流，他们可以做很长时间的演说而不觉得累。这就是为什么有些科学家 80 岁还泡在实验室，有些企业家 70 岁还在演讲，有些歌手终生都在创作。因此，joy 是难以言表的，因为它来自你对深层的自我存在的接受程度。至少从现在起，你可以有意识地去锁定自己在什么时候能感觉到这种 joy。养成生活在快乐中的习惯，你的人生会比较容易地保持明朗的状态。

血脉根基

在北美生活、学习的你会生活在后殖民的文化形态中。要在不同族裔融合的社会中了解自己，给自己明确的定位，就得明白血统的潜在力量。在异国，你可能会感到自己比在中国更是中国人，世世代代流传下来的在血脉当中的积淀会被外化，也会成为你的无形资产和潜在动力。从某种程度上说，家族历史也是帮助你发现自我天赋的捷径。比如，你的祖父母、父母都有什么梦想？他们有什么愿望是被压抑的，是未完成的？家庭成员之间都有什么相似的禀赋？但这并不意味着你就得被前辈定义。比如说，如果你的家人都是医生，你未必就一定喜欢救死扶伤。你的一切仍然由你自己自主选择，但研究家族历史可以给你带来有价值的启发。

比如，我的家人连续四代从事教育事业，对我而言，当老师是顺理成章的事情。但是，正因为我真正尊重这个传统，所以我想拥有一个超乎传统意义上的"教室"，拓宽教育的领域，希望更多的人能获得精神上的启迪。于是，这个选择把我带到了写作领域，使我不仅可以尊重家族传统，还可以将这个传统拓展。反之亦然。比如，如果你的父母都是工程师，而对此传统你相当反叛，成为一个音乐家是你的方向，在这种情况下，家族传统也有同等重要的地位，至少，家族传统让你明白你不想做什么。

血脉是一种无形的财富。所有的传统同时又是无限的，也就是说，它可以被无数次更新、再创造。这可能也是北美文化的优势所在——它给你更新传统的机会，同时又能把各种传统的根基连在一起。理解自己的根基会让你踏实，会减少前进的盲目性，减少迷失自我的可能性，这对生活在北美的各个族裔的人来说都是重要的人生课题。

第三讲　自我价值

　　如果一个人没能实现自己的价值，没能在一生中利用自己的天赋服务于人类，也许他会在生命结束之时有很深的遗憾和挫败感，这也是人们缺乏幸福感的根源所在——没有实现自己的价值。北美文化中公认，打开成功大门的钥匙是找到人生目的（find your life purpose），你会反复听到这句话，而对学生而言，尽早找到自己的人生目标是在学业上领先的关键。往往人们走弯路是因为目标不明确，而清晰的方向能决定明确的目标，有明确的目标会使你更容易成功。所以，要弄清人生目标到底是什么，你要找到以下这些问题的答案："我为什么来到这个世界？""我来这里做什么？""我如何实现自己生命的价值？"你的人生目标也许在童年或少年时代以梦的形式出现，长大以后，如何实现这个梦会逐渐变得现实和明了。也许，你小时候梦想成为一个超级巨星，结果长大以后你成为了一个明星科学家，这就是实现该目标的方式。

　　人生目标与我们存在的本质紧密相连，它与天赋有别。有明确人生目标的人可以在任何困难下保持坚定的方向，并战胜困难。目前，绝大多数在北美上学的中国中小学生都来自殷实家庭，他们衣食无忧，从来不必为物质发愁。物质满足允许他们把精力放在更高层次的需求上。美国心理学家亚伯拉罕·马斯洛（Abraham Maslow）提出的"需要金字塔"指出，人除了基本的生理需要、安全感需要之外，还有精神层面的需要，如对归属感的需要、对自尊的需要、对自我实现的需要①。大部分人的一生都在为上面列举的这三种精神层面的需要，特别是为自我实现的需要而奋斗。在学校，你也会被驱使去寻求自我实现。如果求学只是家长的要求，那么，即使学生努力，其学业成功也很难不受影响。常见的现象是有些孩子选择不喜欢的专业（只因为本专业是家长要求的，或是当前热门的，或是毕业好找工作的），结果大学读得很痛苦，白白浪费了资源，也没法按时毕业。无论你目前在加拿大或者美国的哪一所高中或大学学习，以下的问题也许能够帮助你把学业推向成功。

为何而生

每个人出生都是为了某个特定的使命——这就是为

①黄希庭：《人格心理学》，378 页，杭州，浙江教育出版社，2002。

什么生命绝非毫无意义。整个人生旅程中的每一步前进和后退，都是为了完成那个使命。抑郁症以及其他身心疾病等缺乏快乐现象的出现往往是因为人生使命没有完成，或无法完成。

上述问题对青少年来说并不是太"大"的问题，正相反，年纪越小越容易找到这些问题的答案，它们会让青少年在成年以后少走弯路。如果觉得这些问题与你无关，那么，在北美，你已经比别人至少慢了半拍。世界文化在飞速地融合，世界变得越来越同质化，在这个时代，孩子们经历个人精神上的觉醒和启蒙是非常正常的事。事实上，大部分优秀的青少年都已经有了答案，他们大都已经有了要实现自己理想的决心。

前两讲已经明确，你的天赋是与生俱来的，从某种程度上来说，你不需要"学"，而人生的目标则要求你运用自己的天赋在某一领域造福人类，这就由你和自己的关系转到你和世界的关系。比如，你很善于化解父母之间的纠纷，渴望平静、和谐，那么，你可以将自己调解矛盾的天赋用于给世界带来公正、和平上，也就是说，今后你可能是出色的法官、咨询师等。又如，如果你生来很慷慨，那么，人道主义事业有可能是你今后的道路。思考如何用自己的闪光之处来服务于世界，你会自然得出结论。这也是为什么在大学巨大的学习压力下，有些学生逃避，有些学生被压垮，有些学生盲目选课八年不能毕业，而有些学生却在飞速进步，这跟努力没有关系，而跟动力有关。

自我定义

"我是谁"是一个始终会出现在我们脑海里的问题。如果你的自信心像过山车一样时高时低，这说明你可能还不知道"自己是谁"，或者说，你还没找到真正的自己。比如，有些学生因为得了 A 而自信心飙升，可得了 C 又马上变自卑。这都是他不了解自我，缺乏对自我的明确定位的表现。正如乔普拉在《成功的 7 大精神法则》第 2 章中所说，有些成年人把自我等同于头衔、地位、财富，一旦把"主席""教授"的头衔摘掉，自尊就会受挫，这是自负（ego）的表现。同样，如果你用出众的女友或者富有的父母定义自己，你的自尊也会随时处于危险的境地。真正的自我（self 而非 ego）是很难被伤害的，是不会又卑又亢的，是稳定的。比如，你得了 C，真正自信的学生不会得出"自己很差"的结论，他们会认为，C 只不过说明自己有些地方需要改进，得 C 可以告诉自己如何得到 A，这才是真实自我（self）的声音。

那么，如何定义自己呢？随着时间的推移，你的身份会变，但不变的、定义一个人的存在核心和存在价值的是你的人生目标。关于这一点，我在某种程度上同意乔普拉的总结：你是独一无二的，上天给你某种天赋，你要用自己的这种天赋最大限度地造福他人（见《成功的 7 个精神法则》第 9 章）。比如，你的文化身份有可能从中国人变为华裔美国人，然后有可能又变回中国人，但你的人生目标是不变的。假如你是个舞者，你的人生目标就是通过舞蹈给世界带来美。这样，不管走到世界何处，你都有自己独有的贡献世界的方式，它超越了文化、种族的界限。只要你始终活在自己的人生目标当中，你就会始终是真实的自己。

这里要说明的是，"我是谁"的问题不是一个自我中心主义的问题，而是必须把自我放在最广意义上的"世界"去考量的问题。真正的自我（self）不是自私的，而归根结底是利他主义的。人的价值需要通过帮助他人来实现，否则，不管怎样的天赋都会失去意义。

实现自我

你已经找到的人生目标也许看上去很抽象、很庞大，这样，你就需要在成长过程中将其细化成具体的行动。比如，我小时候发现，我的人生目标是要提升现代文化的质量，这个在脑海中瞬间形成的想法从此再也没有变过。后来，这个很抽象的概念使我对各种哲学理论流派、各种现代主义文学着迷，直到阅读成了我的习惯，直到我遇到了现代主义文学领域的权威。在即将完成我的硕士学业时，我又遇到了美国畅销书作家杰克·坎菲尔德

(Jack Canfield)，他是"心灵鸡汤"系列丛书的最初作者。之后，一连串的转折点把我最终带到了写作的道路上，于是，我小时候抽象的理想变为现实。我的意思是说，看似抽象的人生目标会由我们每天行动的点点滴滴来体现，每一个灵感、每一个努力、每一个决定、每一步前进都与其密切相关。如果感觉理想很遥远、很难实现，那么，你会非常容易放弃——其实大多数人就是这么放弃的。把理想落实到每天的点滴行动中，听从自己的每个灵感，是最有效的激励自己坚持梦想的方式。

对于身处北美的高中生来说，志愿者服务不仅是学校的要求，也是很好的实践途径。做志愿者的真正目的在于，了解你自己是否会在无偿为他人付出的情况下感到快乐，会感到怎样的快乐；你如何从这个过程中更好地了解自己，了解自己的前进方向。许多学生一旦开始从事志愿者工作，就会体会到服务于他人的乐趣，不管自己家里多富有，从志愿者工作中获得的快乐是无价的。这也是申请北美大学时一定会被学校问到的地方，即你怎么理解自己为世界提供的服务。

一旦人生目标确立以后，你会发现，相应的机会也会接二连三地出现，因为宇宙已经知道，你在有意识地塑造未来。除了志愿者服务以外，你可能会突然抓住偶尔冒出的机会登台演讲、登台表演、结识新朋友、参加各种比赛等——抓住各种机会，直到有一天，你发现，自己走过的"地图"都指向同一个方向。这样，对你而言，课余活动、社会活动都不再盲目，而是变得更有深意、更有乐趣，你也最终会将抽象的人生目标转化为现实。

学业目标

　　反复强调人生目标也是因为这是北美教育的关注点。对于北美的高中生、大学生来说，明确人生目标不仅能在本质上促进学业，而且能开发各方面的潜能。北美的教育对个人成长非常有益，它的益处不在于灌输知识，而在于学校的各种资源都在激发你的创造力，帮助你实现自己的理想。

　　如果在进大学之前，你已经明确了今后的方向，那就再好不过了。我教过的一个十年级学生从小患哮喘，她永远都没法忘记那些曾经帮助过、感动过她的医生、护士，她在内心深处想成为一个救死扶伤的人，她觉得自己的使命就是拯救其他儿童的生命。但她在加拿大的成绩并不理想。因此，她这些心底最深层的理想需要外化，需要被他人承认，这样她才会克服在国外学习的压力和恐惧，从而产生对学业的兴趣，产生对自我价值的认同。当她能看见今后要达到的终点的时候，大学，对她而言，就从一个"不得不去的地方"变成了"我想去的地方"。

正因为有明确的人生目标，求学才从被动变为主动。高动机是成就一切事情的关键，从大学申请中，学校会轻而易举地发现你上学的动机怎样，由此推测你是否能顺利完成学业。在中国，学生们可能习惯于被"教"，而北美教育环境需要你把一切事情做在前面，学在前面，而且随时做好超过老师的准备，这也是你在北美胜出的方法。也许，中国传统文化需要你或多或少地掩藏自己，而北美文化则鼓励你毫不谦虚地展现出自己方方面面的个性和优点。

成就篇
自我实现

第四讲　潜能最大化

潜力意味着自我的无限状态尚未完全释放出来。在电影《秘密》中，美国量子物理学家约翰·哈格琳博士（Dr. John Hagelin）告诉我们，"人类大脑只被开发了5%，其中只有1%是受正常教育的结果"。学校只是教会你如何思考，成为推你向前的动力。可是，如何把自己的潜力最大化是你自己需要完成的工作，也是你在北美需要尽早掌握的技能。

要把自己的潜能都挖掘出来，首先得了解大脑是如何运转的。我们的意识领域通过语言文字进行思考，不管是用中文还是英文，只要思维以语言的形式存在，意识（consciousness）就在运转。无意识（unconsciousness）则不同，它以图像、符号的形式，像无声电影一样"思考"。人在入睡以后，意识逐渐关闭，无意识逐渐开始工作，梦就是一系列的图像、行动、象征符号的任意集合。意识和无意识层面都有无限的能量，都能帮你达到目标——如果你知道如何正确运用它们的话。合理地使用语言进行思考和合理地运用非语言进行想象是在北美人尽皆知的开启大脑能力的方法。

明确目标

知道自己到底想要什么是实现各种大大小小目标的前提。通常，人们不敢去追寻自己真正想要达到的目标，是因为他们在心理上没法很快跳出安全区，没法去面对成功到来时候的不知所措和压力。比如，如果真的得了A怎么办？如果真的去了伯克利大学会怎样？等等。在心理上跳出自己的安全区可能会让你感觉不自在，因为你得将自己拔高一大截，周围的环境、别人的反应对你而言都变得陌生。很多在公校就读的中国学生习惯了在英语课上拿C，这就是他们自己的心理安全区，他们认为，自己不是出生在英语国家，所以英语成绩没法得A。很少有学生能突破这种思维惯性，进行逆向思维——正因为我不出生在这里，所以我的英语成绩可以比别人得分高。记住，无意识不以逻辑的、语言的方式思考，而以感觉的、图像的方式思考。害怕拿C，你会得到C；害怕被老师指责，你就会被指责。不如把这种情况调转过来，换一种方式思考，现状会大不一样。

明确目标可以让你少走很多弯路，避免很多盲目性。一方面，压抑自己真实理想的情况会逐渐改变。也许，你想成为一名电影演员，却在读一个科学学位，你把自己的理想藏得很深。也许，你想成为一个音乐家，但父母让你学建筑专业，你可能顺从他们的安排，而错过了自己的梦想。想清楚自己到底有什么愿望，也可以看出你对自己是否忠诚。另一方面，"害怕"的反面也能说明问题。比如，你总是害怕在学校吃午餐时被同学们冷落，那你真正想要的是有关心你的朋友；如果你很害怕演讲，那你其实是希望自己善于演讲；如果你害怕拿不到学位，那你无意识里希望的是拿到学位。学会从大脑中剔除"伪"目标，不要让各种"害怕"的情绪禁锢你前进的脚步，可以帮你确立真实的方向感。

明确的目标导致明确的结果，模糊的目标导致模糊的结果。有些同学说："我想当班上最好的学生。"这是目标，但是不够精确。"最好的学生"是指拿 A 还是A–？是指得 100 分还是 98 分？是指在一个月内还是一周内达到这个目标？有的同学说："我今天要把这个作业做完。""今天"指的是几点？晚上六点还是十点？确立精确的目标会使你的大脑亢奋、有紧迫感，会让你的每个行动都有的放矢。学会确定目标就顺利地打开了成功的大门。量子物理的双缝干涉实验证明，无限的可能性因我们发出意向的改变而改变，这就是为什么明确目标、把有限的精力放在该目标上时会有事半功倍的效果。明确目标是释放潜能的第一步。

视觉化与肯定句

北美小学、高中教室的墙上基本都挂有一块愿景板

(vision board)，这是为了教孩子们学习如何用形象思维能力制定与实现目标。很多人可能有了目标，但很快就将其抛到脑后。于是，对于大部分人来说，梦想也就只是停留在"幻想"阶段而已，大脑的潜能没有被开发出来。在"实现"阶段，有两个重要概念，一是视觉化，二是肯定句，它们是同时运用无意识和意识拓展潜能、在北美人尽皆知的策略。

视觉化是指把目标以图像或者符号的形式放在眼前，直到大脑认为已经达到了该目标。无意识层面基本没有办法从时间上判断什么是过去、什么是将来，这使得在大脑中想象图景极具潜力。比如，你想被某大学录取，你可以把该大学的图片设为电脑桌面；如果你在大学迟迟不能毕业，你可以把别人毕业典礼的图片放在眼前，想象这是你自己的毕业典礼。当无意识"消化"掉这些代表你真实目标的图像的时候，你会更快达到这个目标。

肯定句则是利用语言，即大脑的逻辑部分，从意识层面去干预无意识，以便实现目标。你每时每刻对自己说的话是以语言的形式存在的，代表意识层面的运作。比如，如果你在课堂上很紧张，想"老师可能会叫我的名字"，通常老师接下来就会叫你的名字；如果你想"拿不到学位我妈可能会责怪我"，那你可能真会被责怪。用积极正向的话语去替代消极负向的话语可以改变你对自我的认识。在英语中，说肯定句要注意用一般现在时态、现在完成时态或过去时态，来替代将来时态，暗示大脑事情已经发生或变成常态，大脑会相应地顺应这种变化（注：中文是非时态语言，所以基本不存在这个问题）。比如，我见过很多学生在学校没法毕业，他们越是整天对自己说"毕不了业怎么办"，就越难毕业。而简单地对自己说"我已经毕业了"，这比"我想毕业"或者"我会毕业的"要有效得多。再如，对自己说"我是一个全A学生"比"我会变成一个全A学生"要有效得多。养成说肯定句的习惯并不仅仅是保持积极的态度这么简单，更重要的是，肯定句说出的是一种不受时间约束的信念。

行动力

只懂得合理、有效利用自己的大脑是远远不够的，是否真正实现目标还取决于你是否行动、是否努力，否则将目标视觉化也好，说肯定句也好，都是自欺欺人的废话与妄想。这意味着你不能光嘴上说"我是A等生"，但是行动起来像个C等生；不能整天说自己成功获得了学位，却迟迟不交论文。只有行动能证明你对信念是认真的。当你常说自己都拿A的时候，你会感觉自己聪明了许多，这时候，主动努力会让你学到很晚也不觉得疲惫。也许你原先在课上很少发言，但因为自己在脑海中总是说"我是全A的学生"，有一天你可能突然会举手回答问题，因为这时你已经感觉到自己是班上最好的学生了。原因很简单，因为你已经以一种新的方式在定义和看待自己了，而"所行"必须与"所想"吻合。基本上你可以用这种方法突破任何心理上的安全区和自我限制。

行动力是不可逃避的，行动力的意义远远大于视觉化和肯定句对无意识的影响的意义。如果你在学校发现自己产出很多成果，却仿佛忽视了大脑训练，这是一个好的现象，说明成功对你而言并不只是停留在想象层面，而且你一定能很快看到成绩。例如，有个学生迟迟不能毕业，在转变思路以后，他突然能克服拖延症，在学校图书馆里努力写论文，任何干扰都没法让他分心，因为他所有的精力都集中在一件事情上——当行动力充满大脑时，他反而感觉不到自己是在完成什么目标，而是处于高度沉浸其中的状态。最终，当他获得学位的时候，毕业的信念真正变成有形的事实。当然，这是他应得的，因为他付出过。

自我奖励

对自己有意识的奖励会激励你取得更多的成绩。不管所谓"成绩"有多小，哪怕只是你第一次举手提问，也是值得庆贺的事情。多数情况下，陪读的家长是严厉的角色，但不管有没有家人、朋友在身边鼓励你，自我奖励永远都具备最积极的影响力。你可以买些小礼物，作为给自己的奖赏。如果你想去看电影，那就等拿了 A 再去看，作为对自己的奖励。每一步前进都是奇迹，你会发现，越懂得自我鼓励，你越会遇到更多值得庆祝的事情。

在这方面，父母能帮很大的忙，你可以与支持自己的家长一起合作完成这种良性前进过程。比如，告诉你妈妈，在你写完某个曲子后，再给你买你想要读的那本书。同时，告诉他们，如果你没有做好，也同样给你鼓励。要和亲近的人成为一个团队，他们的反馈是你前进的有效动力。在这方面，我的父母帮了我很大的忙，我习惯于有一丁点儿成绩就告诉他们，然后听到他们积极的肯定。每个孩子都爱听"我为你骄傲"之类的话，父母常说这样的话，孩子会进步得更多。孩子与父母之间应该形成一种奖励系统，而不是惩罚系统，这样，你同父母之间的关系肯定差不了。

或者，你也可以跟亲密朋友达成这种良性的鼓励机制，大家互相鼓励，实现目标。但你必须选择 100% 支持你、态度积极的朋友组成团队，也就是说，不管你成败与否，他们永远鼓励你，站在你这一边，而不是讽刺、挖苦你。反过来，你也可以鼓励、监督他们完成他们的理想或各种目标。真正的好朋友不会整天评价你，指责你，嫉妒你，而是和你一起成长。比如，你们可以达成某个目标后一起去看场电影，开个派对或者做个视频，等等。任何付出所得到的任何奖赏都会激发你的内在，让你爆发自己的小宇宙。结果是，你一定会更优秀、更有成就，也会得到更珍贵的友谊。

第五讲 竞争的最高境界是不竞争

很多学生说，来北美读高中就是为了避免高考的压力。但来了以后才发现，北美的竞争也很激烈，只不过这里的竞争是以另一种形式呈现的。在北美的学校，你更多时候是同自己竞争，这意味着你必须练就追求卓越的本领。根据经验，胜出的悖论就在于，最佳的竞争是"不与他人竞争"。道家思想中的"道"在西方的修辞手法里基本等同于反讽（irony），它告诉我们，最无敌的战士最了解对手，但不会把时间浪费在同别人竞争上，可能他唯一的对手就是他自己，或者用尽全力做最卓越的自己，这才是"无敌"。前几讲的内容已经足够让你鹤立鸡群，这一讲则会告诉你怎样解决竞争的问题。

一个在各种情况下总能胜出的人善于从失败中总结教训，做真实的自己，全力以赴走自己的路。把注意力放在塑造自我上面，放在自己能做的事情上，你就不会总把自己跟别人比，不会嫉妒别人有什么，不会被旁人左右，反而总能得到尊敬和欣赏。

生来为赢

我深信，每个人生来就是赢家，不管你后来的经历如何。你经历的挫折越多，你得到的知识也越多，你学到的任何经验都可以增强自己的实力。比如，我小时候的"学习障碍"反而让我的左脑发展得更好，因为大量阅读、专业批评理论训练增强了我的逻辑思维能力。毕业后，我遇到很多有类似"学习障碍"的高中生，他们在学校相当有挫败感，我只想说，这种困难是有益的，它们并不意味着所谓的"失败"。

面对竞争的时候，你需要仔细研究自己后，填上某个空白——某个没人想到、没人涉足的领域。在这个充满无限可能性的世界里，一定有什么空白需要你的智慧、才华去填补，所以，当你选择一种独一无二的方式去填补一个独一无二的空白的时候，就很少有人能跟你竞争。正因为在这个世界上你是独一无二的，是没人能替代的，所以，只要你发挥自己独有的个性，你就自然会赢。换句话说，世界上总有什么事情是只有你能做的，所以没人能超过你。只有你自己才是自己真正的竞争对手，任何胜利都是自我的成长。

胆量与亲和力

competitive 竞争听上去残酷，它也许是大多数孩子都想逃避的事情。但有意思的是，你越逃避竞争，反而越容易面临激烈的竞争，而更多情况下，最大的所谓"敌人"其实就是你自己。在北美，你需要时刻保持一种勇士的心态，不要抗拒、规避竞争激烈的环境，要主动迎接各种挑战。最好的赢家首先会接受挑战，然后再去弄清事情该怎么做——这是赢家的心态。有个学生还没有上十一年级就觉得阅读一本英语小说是一件很恐怖的事情，总觉得自己没准备好。我们的常规思维往往是，在我们不知道该如何做一件事情时，我们会拒绝去做，但是，极具竞争力的人通常先相信自己可以做，再去着手学习如何做。大多数时候，我们面临的最大阻碍是自己大脑中的消极思维，而赢家总是有勇气面对困难和未知局面。

真正懂得竞争、有实力的学生不会看上去颐指气使，而是有相当稳定的自信心和亲和力。有些时候，竞争会变成一种保卫自我的战场，其他人可能用打击你或者否定你来抬高自己，也可能嫉妒你的天赋，那些通过降低别人抬高自己水准的人反而最容易失败。真正的赢家不会把时间和精力浪费在别人怎么看自己上。在强者如林的环境里，你只需要考虑怎么走自己的道路，享受自己的时间，和支持、珍惜你的人为伍，远离学校那些嫉妒、刺激你的人，这样，你最终会赢，因为胜者的智慧在于他们只把时间花在发展自我和提高自我上。

减少负能量

你向世界发出正能量，正能量一定会回来找你；你向世界发出负能量，负能量也一定会回来找你。如果你想成为佼佼者，你就要学会支持和鼓励身边的人成为佼佼者，这是种良性能量循环。比如，学校里，有人在背后议论你，但你不要反过来议论别人；别人小看你，但你不要小看别人；别人欺负你，但你在强大了以后不要反过来欺负别人。"冤冤相报"不是一种积极的能量互动，它对自己和自己周围的人都没好处。人只有处于爱的状态、贡献的状态、支持的状态，才会更优秀。因为这些状态会使你无论走到哪里，总能把光明带给别人，同时，你自己会积攒越来越多的正能量。智慧的人知道你给予世界的光明越多，得到的光明也就越多。

所以，成为胜者的重要一点在于，你要学会保护自己的正能量场，养成屏蔽任何消极因素的习惯，更要养成随时给予他人关心、爱和温暖的习惯，养成帮助别人的习惯，养成付出的习惯。这样，久而久之，没人能伤害到你的光环，这是不与别人竞争的无敌之处。你拥有的光环越大，越能赢得别人的拥护和鼓励。

从容胜利

在北美，你大可不必太谦虚，而要习惯随时接受、感谢别人对你的赞美评价，学会感恩。这不是让你违背、放弃自己作为中国人的一面，而是让你在尊重自己民族传统的同时，也创造新的自我。

有一部分中国学生性格上非常内敛，这些学生就更不能隐藏自己，而要学会让别人看到自己的光芒。我不认为谦逊和自信是矛盾的，你的个人力量和自信来源于你知道自己"是谁"，并做真实的自己。害羞和内向有可能会阻碍你发展，因为身处英语文化的人是很直接的，不太懂得含蓄，不太懂得读潜台词。如果你总是谦逊，常说自己还不够好，那么，没人会认为你够好，受逻各斯中心主义影响的文化基本只认话语的力量。在接受你所处的班集体的奖励时，你也不必太低调。你应该随时准备接受大大小小的成功和奖励，这会从本质上改变你的思维方式和气场。从更深层面来说，随时准备从容大方地接受各种胜利是肯定自我价值的表现，说明你尊重自己对世界的点滴贡献，并且认为自己的付出值得赞许和奖励。

第六讲 赢在艰难时

中国家长总是对孩子过分保护，比如，在多伦多有几千个陪读的家长。但是，爱心呵护和物质资源并不一定能造就孩子毫无挫折的人生。不管你身处哪个人生阶段，该出现的磨砺还是会出现，这很正常。磨砺的出现不是你突然倒了霉，而是因为你眼前有个光明的未来，只是你当前需要成长。如果你目前心情不佳，因为遭受损失、经历失恋等正处于低谷期，那么，你更需要知道，这些事情的发生其实都是有原因的，它们都可以促使你改变。

如何面对挫折，可以证明你到底是怎样的人，这能把你跟别人区分开来。也许你很努力，但还总是取得 C 的成绩；也许你训练了很久，但还是输了一场比赛；也许你很爱自己的女友，但她还是离开了你……这些都很正常。真正的强者能理解各种事情发生的必然性，看到任何事情背后潜藏的财富，然后重新崛起。

聚焦信念

　　信念是指你相信什么。你相信的不一定是什么重大的概念，它可以小到你相信自己是聪明的，相信自己是可以完成一件事的。在遇到困难的时候，你的信念会被挑战，会被检验。比如，你在一次小测验中没有考好，分数很低，于是，你开始怀疑自己还是不是班上最好的学生，这种自我怀疑很正常。但是，有信念的年轻人懂得怎么扭转这种状况。你有能力把任何害怕的心理，如"我已经不再是最好的"，变成对自己的信任，如"这个测验只是告诉我在哪里需要改进"。小事大事上都是如此。胜者只花时间强化自己的信念，而不是放大自己内心的恐惧。

　　恐惧是在期待失败。放大恐惧是人们不知不觉容易犯的错误，当一个人害怕一件事情的时候，他的意识会长时间地停留在这件事上面，甚至多年都无法消退。比如，害怕犯同样一个错误，结果你会反反复复犯这个错误，犯了很多年还在犯同样的错误；害怕受伤害的人结果反而总是受伤害。恐惧心理的出现是因为你在某方面缺乏知识——你通常不会害怕熟悉的事情。比如，经常做饭的人走到哪里都不怕做饭这件事，经常演讲的人走到哪里都不怕没东西讲。克服恐惧的方法是，尽快掌握相关的知识，不管是专业知识，还是心理学常识。你首先要有坚定的信念，相信自己能搞定某件让你害怕的事；然后，通过努力获取知识，你就可以彻底消除恐惧。当再遇到类似情况的时候，就没有什么能难倒你了。

锁定远景

在我们的成长中，小的困难几天就过去了，而有些困难会持续地、长时间地折磨你、考验你，让你长期处于挫败状态。出现这种状态不一定是因为你害怕，但你可能很难看到希望或转机。大部分人都会长期纠结于某一个困难，直到觉得精疲力竭。比如，有的同学在学校长期交不到朋友，感觉自己像一个局外人（wallflower）；有些同学长期克服不了小时候的某个阴影。即使面临这种情况，你最终仍然可以扭转局面，只要你学会把注意力放在远景目标上，而不是放在当前的困难上。远景是说你的大方向，你要时刻提醒自己往哪里走，这可以给你带来力量和克服困难的勇气。

煎熬的时刻是一定会过去的，看不见希望的时候反而说明希望近在咫尺。举个例子，J. K. 罗琳（J. K. Rowling）在写《哈利·波特》第一部的时候，人生处在低谷，但是她把所有精力都放在自己的人生目标上，写自己喜欢的故事，而不是把精力放在当前的困难上。《哈利·

波特》后来的成功世人皆知：罗琳在抑郁症的基础上建立了自己的想象王国。当你的人生也出现类似的"黑点"，让你觉得进入"死胡同"的时候，你反而需要把注意力从眼前的困难中转移出来，把注意力放在大方向——你要到达的终点上，放在应该做的事情上，然后朝着这个方向努力，困难就会过去。这些使人迅速前进的困难不是灾难，而是有益的帮助。人们总是在最困难的时候也前进得最多。

被拔高的乐趣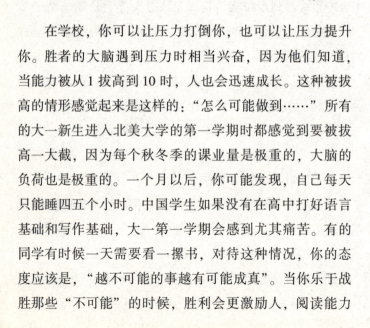

在学校，你可以让压力打倒你，也可以让压力提升你。胜者的大脑遇到压力时相当兴奋，因为他们知道，当能力被从 1 拔高到 10 时，人也会迅速成长。这种被拔高的情形感觉起来是这样的："怎么可能做到……"所有的大一新生进入北美大学的第一学期时都感觉到要被拔高一大截，因为每个秋冬季的课业量是极重的，大脑的负荷也是极重的。一个月以后，你可能发现，自己每天只能睡四五个小时。中国学生如果没有在高中打好语言基础和写作基础，大一第一学期会感到尤其痛苦。有的同学有时候一天需要看一摞书，对待这种情况，你的态度应该是，"越不可能的事越有可能成真"。当你乐于战胜那些"不可能"的时候，胜利会更激励人，阅读能力以不可想象的速度迅速增长就是这么实现的。

　　如果你已经进入大学，但还没有体验过这种被拔高的感觉，说明你可能在原地踏步，说明在期末的时候你会比别人更焦躁。我们前面说过，你已经找到了自己的方向，而北美的大学就是帮助你实现目标的土壤。锻炼拔高能力就像锻炼肌肉一样，是一个集训过程，如果你很难做出改变，跳出自己的安全区，如果你抗拒这种拔高过程，这只能让你被淘汰得更快。有些同学会用逃避的心态去面对庞大的作业量，第一学期结束的时候，可能面临三门课退课的情况。所谓的作业量在教授看来是很轻的，到第二年你自己回头看时，也觉得"大一时候的课业量不重"。面临满负荷的工作量时，保持强者的乐观态度，告诉自己愿意接受任何挑战，你会不知不觉挖掘出自己想象不到的潜力。

自我教育

　　首先，我们的一生需要不少人生导师，但通常他们只是出现在你生命中的某一段特定时间、某个特定领域，他们启发我们，然后离开。而那个永远可以指导你的人生导师是你自己，这意味着你得养成阅读、随时更新知识的习惯。刚进入维多利亚大学时，这里的图书馆很让我满意，整个三层收藏的都是人文类书籍。但在做研究的时候，我深深感觉这个图书馆已经远远不够用了，我需要向北美各地的图书馆搜罗资料。我还发现，很多我想阅读的东西并不在图书馆，这些东西要么太新，要么不太学术，大脑的不满足感让我涉猎图书馆以外的各种资源，这使我可以随时更新知识，保持前进的步伐。

其次，大家还必须知道的一点是，教授或老师虽然是专家，但他们并不一定通晓所有知识，因为专长可能本身就意味着对思维的约束，专家们的视野反而不一定开阔，换句话说，专家只是很小一个领域的专家。许多同学习惯于依赖教授和老师传授的知识，而没有机会发展独立思考能力和探索能力。如果你发现你知道教授不知道的知识时，有可能你会很快找到自己的研究领域。这就是为什么自我教育很重要。在北美，你不需要依赖权威，而要学会独立思考，学会用自己的声音建立自己的权威。

最后，十有八九，有一天你会发现，学到最后连大学本身也是局限，已经不能满足你的需求。那时，你也应该相信自己的直觉，继续引导自己发展新的技能，开拓新的疆域。也许天才一般的你，没有哪种教育可以与你百分百契合。大学的作用仅仅在于把你推向你应该去的地方。所有成功的人都知道，自己才是自己最好的老师，而且是终生免费的。

实践篇
自我训练

训练一 批判性思维

批判性思维是在英语学术环境中思考、写作、阅读都需要的基本工具。它从简单到复杂有几个阶段。值得注意的是，批判性思维经常被人误解，非常容易被滥用，也非常容易成为负能量的源头。一个训练有素的大脑懂得如何"有控制"地使用批判性思维，也懂得批判性思维的最高境界其实是创新。在这里，根据经验，只介绍中国学生在高中阶段急需的、实用的方法。

批判性思维入门

中国学生在高中从非母语英语课程（ESL）转向学术英语的学习过程中，发展批判性思维（critical thinking）是最大的障碍，这也是所有学生都要渡过的难关。学会用批判性思维思考不是一蹴而就的过程，它需要一定的时间去训练，这对中国学生如此，对其他族裔的学生也是一样。

在初学阶段，同学们在掌握批判性思维时，需要"发现"各种问题，要学会提出"有价值"的问题，如逻辑上的漏洞、逻辑上模糊的地方。提出"有价值"的问题、使用批判性思维的目的是为了将思路完善。下面我任意摘取我写过的草稿中的两句话，来看批判性思维是怎样运用的：

【例1】The entire framework of Julian's paper is very clear and well arranged. However, it seems that the introduction part could be shortened in some way.

【分析】读者应该能够一眼看出这句话有什么问题。首先，作为评论，最好不要说 it seems that（似乎），因为如果作者自己都飘忽不定的话，其论述很难做到有说服力。其次，in some way（在某些方面）是指 in "what" way（在哪些方面）？这里所指很不明确，最好根据上下文内容替换掉 some。再次，这句话在句法、措辞上也不算到位，可以改为：

Julian's paper is well structured. The introduction part, however, could be more succinct.

再看一个关于重复的例子（摘自一位同学的草稿，在此匿名）：

【例2】Every kind of emotion weight same to human. There is no such an emotion that means less or more important than each other.（Anonymous）

【分析】除了明显的语法错误以外，这里的主要问题是第二句话重复第一句话的内容。中国学生常犯这样的错误，即反复重复同一个意思，觉得第一次没有讲清楚，所以要再重复讲一遍，这违背了线性逻辑的原则。所以，要尽量一次讲清楚，避免不必要的重复。上面的两句话可以直接合并为一句话：

All kinds of human emotions are equally important.

下面是一个逻辑含糊的问题（摘自一位同学的草稿，在此匿名）：

【例3】The one who killed the winner of the struggle within animals was Pi who replaced tiger.（Anonymous）

【分析】这句话非常令人费解，读者应该能看出由于句法缠绕在一起引起的表达歧义。winner 指的是谁？animals 指的是哪些，包括 tiger 还是不包括？读者要仔细看半天才能发现 one 指代的是谁。逻辑清晰意味着你不能给读者造成任何阅读上的障碍。作为英语作者，你在上十二年级以后大部分写的都是劝说文（persuasive essay）——用你的观点说服别人，这就要求你书写的清晰度和可读性。这句话大致可以改为：

In the second story, Pi kills the winner of the battle and becomes the "tiger."

由此可见，批判性思维的目的不在于批评别人，更不是种愤世嫉俗（cynicism）的情绪，而是在于改进逻辑的不完善之处。发现不完善之处是为了让我们的思想更有价值，让我们的大脑更高效、更多产。这归根结底也是培养发现和解决问题的能力。所有对批判性思维的运用都不应该是消极的，而应该是建设性的、富有创造力的。学术界需要批判性思维这个基本工具来产出有价值的思想，推动各个学科前进。

掌握批判性思维不等于右脑要处于劣势，或者停止工作。相反，右脑的想象力、感知力能为逻辑思维提供很多帮助。我认为，创造力是最高级阶段的批判性思维。从思考的速度上来说，直觉、想象、灵感远远比逻辑思维快，逻辑思维需要通过时间过程从 A 到 Z，但对于右脑思维者而言，从 A 到 Z 是一瞬间的事情。比如，当你写作文时，某个观点瞬间出现在脑海，但是，用逻辑证明、收集论据、完善论证过程需要一定的时间。中国学生的优势在于，他们通常具有较强的灵感、直觉、悟性这些非语言、非逻辑思维，这往往让他们得出正确的观点，对于这个优势，中国学生要学会合理利用。所以，要发展批判性思维和线性逻辑，右脑的支持也不能忽略。

避免批判"精神"

批判性思维是一种工具而非一种"精神"。事实上，这是西方批判性思维极度发展后悬崖勒马的情况，也是西方的文化前沿出现向东方文化靠拢的趋势的原因。思维训练有素的人，尤其懂得"有控制地"使用批判性思维。有的学生在北美学习成绩优异，批判性思维能力娴熟，但同时也养成了停不下来、过分思考的习惯。习惯用英语思考的学生一定有这样的体会：大脑以语法的形式思考停不下来，思绪像关不住的水龙头一样流淌。他们写的作文也通常趋于冗长，容易超过字数限制。因为线性逻辑可以一直持续不间断，因此，对这些学生来说，他们需要掌握的能力是学会简洁表达，学会产出有价值的思想，把时间花在有意义的问题上。

批判性思维让人容易发现和提出问题，也容易使人变得消极，总是看到缺陷。很多同学在越学越好的同时，性格也变得越来越消极，越来越爱挑自己和别人以及任何事情的毛病。在学术领域也是如此。有很大作为的人也有可能时时处处都在批判，而且对此他们很难控制自己。这也是西方思想界早就意识到的问题。拉美西斯·福恩马约尔（Ramsés Fuenmayor）在《系统思维与批评 I. 什么是批评？》（"Systems Thinking and Critique. I. What is Critique?"）①一文中阐述了西方哲学史上演进的三种批评，即"教条式批判（dogmatic critique）""内部批判（immanent critique）""超越式批判（transcendental critique）"。教条式批判是最专制和原始的状态，意思是

---

① Fuenmayor, Ramsés. "Systems Thinking and Critique. I. What is Critique?" *Systemic Practice and Action Research*, 3.6 (1990)：524–44. *SpringerLink*.

"我说对的就是对的"。内部批判可能是所谓"消极"的来源，即双方互相否定，互相挑漏洞，争论无休无止。批判性思维的最高境界是超越式批判，指在不否定某观点的前提下的无限创新。

初学批判性思维的学生容易停留在内部批判的阶段。这时候的你非常容易找到任何事情的缺陷，从而发展出对任何事情的消极态度。如果你感觉自己批判性思维能力增长，但同时也对自己和他人更苛刻，这说明你的思维能力还要继续升级，即要达到超越式批判，要在不否定的前提下产出创造力。当上了大学，思维通过大量阅读、写作迈上新一层台阶的时候，你就会发现，成熟的批判性思维既不是负能量的，也不是重复循环的思维，而是富有创造性和建设性的思维。在超越式批判思维阶段，你应该把精力集中在扩充当前的知识上，而不是集中在如何否定它上，你的感觉应该是"有更多的值得去挖掘"，而不是"这是错的"。通常，在成熟的英语学术环境下，一个已经学会思考的人没有所谓的批判"精神"。真正处于最高阶段的批判性思维注重悉心产出对世界有益的观点。

训练二　学术写作

从高中起，学术英语写作已是学生必须掌握的技能，是上大学前必备的技能，这个基础没有打好，完成大学作业会有相当的困难。学术英语写作可能包括对比文、劝说文等，以及大学水平以上的各类论文。而这类写作都遵循一定的规律和固定模式。比如，最常用的劝说文是要求你用自己独立的论点去说服读者；文体应该正式，使用学术用语而不是口语化语言；从文章的框架能看出逻辑是否顺畅。以下讲解及例证仅适用于劝说文。

基本结构和线性逻辑

学术英语写作的基本结构为：introduction（前言）+ body paragraph(s)（主体段）+ conclusion（总结）。我们都知道，不管篇幅多长，第一段都是 introduction，它的内部结构为论点加上你通过什么步骤去证明它。introduction 在五百字左右的短论文中通常是一段，在几千字的论文中可能是几段。但有经验的研究者都知道，introduction 反而是最后完成的，特别是当论文在五千字以上的时候。在写文学评论的文章时，一篇论文的逻辑起点一般是文学作品中的论据或者说是例子，从例子推出一个观点放在段首作为该段的主题句，再从若干 body paragraphs 中推出conclusion，最后自然而然地推出文章的论点，然后再写你的 introduction。你的论文要求字数越多，可能越需要在草稿中以这样的顺序写。

在文学评论的文章中，每一个 body paragraph 的结构也遵循一定的模式。第一句一定是主题句 topic sentence，即该段的核心论点；然后是证明它的论据和小说/戏剧/诗歌中的例子，以及关于为什么这个例子证明了主题句中的观点的分析；最后写一句话的结论。大多数学生在写这类作文的时候，容易犯一个错误，那就是，忽略对论据的分析和解释，他们期待老师能读懂这些例子，能自然而然地理解例子与主题句的关系。学术类写作不能让读者问你"这是什么意思"，而是要每句话都精确、有说服力。另一个常见的错误是，段尾不写总结句。很多同学认为，总结句就是对主题句的简单重复，或者认为，总结句可写可不写。总结句必须要写，否则，段落看起来是未完成的，给读者的感觉是论述还要继续下去。

所有学习英语写作的学生都会问一个问题，即"怎么写最终的 conclusion"。不管是一段的总结句，还是一篇论文的总结段，conclusion 都只回答一个问题，那就是"so what"？它强迫你思考以上论述的目的、意义何在，花时间写这么多是为了什么。它不是对论点的简单重复，而是比introduction更深刻。同时，写总结段是对以上逻辑思维是否顺畅的检验，如果写不出总结，答不出"so what"这个问题，那就说明前面的逻辑是模糊的或者混乱的。相反，熟练掌握文学批评写法的同学如果能自然写出结论，那就说明结论之前的论述是有效的，是可以信服的。在写结论的时候，中国学生通常犯的另一个错误是引出新观点、新话题。结论中忌讳出现新的信息点，因为根据线性逻辑的规律，出现新的信息，说明文章还要继续扩展解释它，也就是说，论述没有结束。

我们多次提到线性逻辑，在英语环境中，它是思维的工具。它看似抽象，但其实很容易掌握。线性逻辑就像火车车厢一样，节节相连。比如，你写一个句子 A，下一句话 B 是对 A 中信息的解释和扩展，再下一句 C 进一步扩展 B 中的信息点，依此类推，直到总结句不再给出"新的信息"为止，句子之间一环扣一环完成论述。初学学术写作的学生容易把论述写成绕圈圈，翻来覆去讲一个观点，感觉逻辑拧在一起。逻辑思维能力培养起来以后，这种情况就会好转。我们来看下面的例子（摘自我的一篇草稿）：

【例 1】Rather than creating mysteriousness or ambiguity, it is these contradictions of his personality that disclose his unresolved Oedipus complex（A），the ongoing libidinal power of which drives him to seek for an ideal father（B）. For fatherless Coriolanus（C）, Menenius does not fit for the position of the father（D）…

【分析】我们来看一下这两句中的线性逻辑是怎么展开的。在 A 句中，第一个重要的信息是 contradictions of his personality，它在解释前半句中的 mysteriousness or ambiguity。A 句中的第二个重要信息是 unresolved Oedipus complex，其后的同位语 the ongoing libidinal power 和整个 B 句都在进一步解释 unresolved Oedipus complex。注意，B 句的结尾是 an ideal father，于是下一句一定是对 an ideal father 的展开，然后 D 句又引出新的信息点 Menenius 这个人物名，依此类推，下一句肯定是要解释 Menenius 为什么不是一个 father 形象。线性逻辑就是如此简单。

我们再看下面这个例子中的线性逻辑是怎么断掉的（暂且忽略该同学这里犯的语法错误）：

【例 2】The speaker of "The Road Not Taken" thinks that the two roads appear in front of him are the difficult choices or changes in people's lives（A）. I also find that it seems like both poems are to describe different views in different seasons（B）.（Anonymous）

【分析】这是初学论述的同学经常遇到的问题——A 句和 B 句之间跳跃太大，没有紧密联系，思路太随心所欲。A 句中给出的关键信息是 two roads, difficult choices, changes in people's lives。由于 two roads 已经解释过了，下句应该直接扩展的内容是 difficult choices，然后再解释 changes in people's lives。而作者跳过这两个内容，在 B 句中给出其他陌生的信息点 different views 和 different seasons。这给 A、B 两句之间造成了逻辑上的鸿沟。注意，没有展开解释的内容不能跳过，不能想到哪儿写到哪儿。B 句如果要往下展开，那么首先应该写 both poems 是哪两首诗，是什么样的 different views 和什么样的 different seasons，依此类推。对于语法已经基本过关的同学，在写作下笔的时候要注意逻辑的缜密和连贯，做到无懈可击。

如果自己在学校不知道如何拓展该能力，还有其他的方式可以帮助你。一是，雇一个专业的编辑或者老师帮你修改一个段落，让他们帮你理清你真正要表达的内容，你从中可以学习如何把混乱的逻辑变成线性逻辑，他们修改得越多，你的写作能力就进步得越快。如果你目前在大学，可以使用图书馆的写作中心（Writing Center），每个大学图书馆都有这类服务，在此你可以明确自己写作的问题所在。二是，注意老师发给你的阅读文章（评论性而非英语文学作品）是如何架构的，看每段的逻辑是如果展开、如何结束的。

完美的作文都不是一次写成的，修改作文是每个学生进入大学前必须学会的技能。学会修改作文的技能不仅有用，而且会让你的批判性思维能力更强，使你发现问题和解决问题的能力更强。在大学有个大家都知道的常识，那就是，没有编辑校对过的乱七八糟的草稿最好不要上交。大学也一定会有同学互评（peer review）之类的作业，就是同学之间要互相提问题、互相修改内容。你能发现自己写作中的错误，就能发现别人写作中的问题。peer review 是提高批判性思维的有效方法，几乎每个老师都会用。

高效率的写作步骤是有了观点以后先写 outline，也就是文章的骨架，反复修改以后再写草稿（draft），然后反复修改草稿的逻辑漏洞。这是最省时间的方法，否则，你会在修改时才发现要重写，因为你可能洋洋洒洒写到最后思路才清楚。英语论述文忌讳洋洋洒洒（创造性写作除外），而是注重思路清楚、简洁、一目了然。所以，完善提纲后再下笔，能避免在修改上做大量的无用功。反复修改的过程可以让你不断发现新问题，这是批判性思维增强的过程，久而久之，你读他人作文时的批评能力也会增强，容易发现其中的逻辑漏洞，提出好问题。高中 level 4 的作文和大学得 A 的作文一定是被修改过无数次的。如果在高中就养成修改任何文本的好习惯，那么，在大学你会比别人更容易完成篇幅较长的论文。

写作的最后一个步骤叫润色（polish），也就是说，在修改逻辑错误、确保论述成立以后，你需要修改所有的语法错误、拼写错误、标点错误、句法结构错误，以及用词不当、表达不妥的地方。许多学生以为修改就是查语法错误，结果校对完语法，最后仍然把满篇的逻辑错误交上去了。也就是说，你在完善语言使之成为符合标准的英语之前，一定要先改内容、完善思路。

拖延症和完美主义

拖延症是指把应该做的事情往后推，不拖到截止日期（deadline）不动手的习惯，这在学生中极其普遍。每个学生都或多或少地有拖延症，重要的是怎么解决它。北美大学对待 deadline 的态度是很神圣的，每门课的老师都有对延期交作业的惩罚制度，没有十万火急的情况教授是不会给学生延期（extension）的。我曾见过得到了extension 但还在拖延交不上作业的学生，这种情况的后果是极其严重的。轻度的拖延症表现为，比如，deadline前一天才动手做，非要等到最后一刻才着急。拖延其实是心理上的害怕，学生们一般都知道 deadline 的严肃性，但越怕做不完越往后拖。简单的解决办法是，给自己定一个更早一点儿的 deadline，这样，当真正的 deadline 到来时，你就不用再手忙脚乱了。有拖延症情况的学生没必要害怕，因为害怕也解决不了任何问题，只要学会提前做好计划就好。

　　拖延症总是与完美主义有关。极端的完美主义者花大量时间思考，但就是不动笔。越想写下完美的论述，就越是写不出一个字。完美主义会阻碍人的思维，特别是逻辑的正常运转，理论上说，所有的逻辑都是有漏洞的，也就是说，没有所谓的绝对完美的逻辑，就连已经发表的文章中也可能会有漏洞。不管你有多仔细，左脑思维总会留下逻辑空白。所以，要想克服完美主义，就得不管第一稿有多糟糕，先写了再说，然后给自己留下充足的时间修改——行动永远大于一切空想。

训练三　英语语音

如果英语是你的第二语言，你的发音有多标准其实是你的主观"选择"。每个人都绝对可以跟英语是母语的人发音一样标准。也许有的英语老师说，你们不可能跟英语是母语的人一样有标准发音，那是因为他们自己做不到。只要你想做到语音标准，就可以做到。

改变思维限制

习得标准的发音最关键的不一定是语音训练，而是正确的心态。如果你认为这是容易的事，它就一定会变简单。很多学生学了很多年英语，即使在国外待了很多年，语音还是有比较明显的问题，原因是他们根深蒂固地认为，自己没有出生在这里，所以不可能说出标准的英语。结果，"不能说标准的英语"就成了他们自己有意识的选择。反过来，如果你总是对自己说"我的发音是标准的"，你的语音就逐渐会往标准的方向发展。

有个研究方向叫二语习得，我个人认为，在心理上始终把外语当"外语"来看待，本身就是自己对自己的思维、能力和意识的禁锢。反过来，采用逆向思维，把外语作为另一个母语来看待，就像婴儿天然获得语言一样，外语就变得不那么难学。婴儿从来不会在跟母亲说话时觉得"这是外语，我有困难"。你可以学得很快，不用想"我不是婴儿，学不了第二母语"。前面已经讲过，我们的潜能是无限的，我们思维的局限才是真正的局限。学好一门外语要冲破根深蒂固的意识限制，那就是不要把它当成外语，而要把它当成另一种母语，用自然的方式学习。

如果你能拥有正确的心态，你就已经给自己帮了大忙。练习的第一个窍门是模音。我的这个经验来自于青岛科技大学 VOC 电台延续多年的传统训练模式，当年在这里读书时，我有幸能在电台老师前辈们的专业指导下练习语音。由于右脑可以很快习得新事物，当你听到一个发音，就模仿它直到你的发音和标准模式一模一样为止。最有效的方法是每天将自己的发音录下来，再回放，听哪里有缺陷，再改进，再回放。这样的反复训练可以帮你有意识地矫正每个发音。目前网络上也有很多类似矫正发音的软件，有的可以给你打分，监测你的进步，我认为这是很方便的训练方法，同学们大可下载这类软件，自己坚持练习，持之以恒。

第二个窍门是学一点语音知识。已经在英语环境中的你，虽然模仿能让你很快地学习语音，但是，有时候你仍然不知道怎么将一些音发到位，比如 l, th, s, a 等。这时候，你需要找到英语发音器官图（在网上用任何搜索引擎都可以找到），观察舌头、牙齿、上颚的确切位置，它们如何互相配合共同造就一个音。10 年级以下的同学可以找当地学校的 ESL 老师帮你矫正语音，学习每个音是怎么通过精确的位置变成精确发音的。另外，中文和英语的发音位置是不同的，英语更多用的是鼻腔后部的肌肉力量。如果你的发音位置无法靠后，或者说发音位置跟中文一致，就容易造成语音不标准的情况。语音的练习贵在用心和坚持，不要让某个小小的、含混不清的发音一直伴随你——把它解决在当下。

既然已经置身于英语国家，你的发音就应该有飞速的进步。但是，事实不一定如此。很多家长很困惑：怎么从小学就出来读书了，英语还说成那样？不是在英语环境中进步应该快一点吗？不是只要跟英语是母语的人相处，英语就应该提高很多吗？导致这些状况的原因是，除了学生缺乏一定的自律能力以外，很多学生没有得到正确的引导，学校对语音不准的情况持宽容的态度，学生自己心理上也觉得不在乎；还有的学生练习语音难以持之以恒。其实，在青少年时期出国的学生，在无意识中对很多困难是逃避的，越逃避就越难进步。像我之前说过的，你完全可以引导自己，让自己成就这件小事。在当地雇一个语音教练手把手教你，也是一个好方法。

语音不是学校要求的项目，但它仍然很重要，应该至少给自己一两个月的时间进行训练，然后不要再让这件事阻碍你前进。

百分百自信

　　语音标准可以在很多方面提高你的自信。你可能会发现，标准的语音可以使你想要学习更多新知识，更有勇气去交新朋友，你的个性会更开朗，更愿意承担责任。英语语音不好不应该成为你成功的阻力，更不应该成为你今后反复述说的故事，因为现在你已经知道自己有无限的潜能，可以克服这个简单的障碍。

　　如果你认为自己是天才，你就能成为天才。如果你觉得自己能实现不可能的事，你就一定能达到别人眼里的不可能。如果你能看扁一个困难，这个困难就会变小。如果你觉得自己是了不起的，那么你就一定有什么地方出类拔萃。如果你认为自己是个奇迹，那你就是别人眼里的奇迹。你会成为自己的选择。事实上，每个人都值得拥有自己梦想的一切，这就是为什么你应该无条件地自信。

训练四　大学申请

　　在十二年级末申请大学的过程中，你会发现以上知识都能派上用场。你在准备申请材料的过程中遇到的各种问题都是在检验你：有没有给自己明确的定义，有没有掌握基本的技能，是否具备所有进入大学的条件。如果你已经为自己的学业打下坚实的基础，那么，申请大学的过程一定轻松、有趣。

让大学要定你

　　在大学申请中，你要有很强的竞争力才能胜出。来自世界各地的成千上万的人都在申请同一个项目，你跟别人有什么不同？时间应该花在研究自己而不是你的对手身上。独有的声音会让你从人群中脱颖而出，因为世界上没有人经历过你的人生，世界上也没有第二个人会复制你的人生目标。是你自己的人生塑造了你的兴趣、才华和梦想，把你带到了目前想申请的大学。

　　通常一定会被问到的问题有：你怎么定义自己？为什么申请这个学校？如何为该校做出贡献？你将如何服

务于自己的社区或人类发展？如果你对这些问题都有了比较清楚的答案，那么你基本可以应付学校对以上问题的不同问法。让学校觉得没你不行，这说明你很稀有，对自我有清楚的界定，可以对世界做出很大的贡献。这样，你就可以比别人更快地得到录取通知。

如果说在申请上有什么秘诀的话，那就是你要充分了解自己，懂得自己的价值和方向。如果某个学校没有给你通知书，那可能是它的损失。记住，优秀的你一定会从一堆通知书中，选一个自己最喜欢的。

当你回答学校问题或者参加学校面试的时候，学校绝对能从你的"语气"中一目了然地看到你的自信和真实性。

自信的语气可以表现出，你对自己的目标很明确。很多同学的申请材料看起来是这样的："我也不知道我要不要上这所大学。""我家人让我上这所大学。"这种空洞又模棱两可的语气最能说明你还没有准备好。如果你自己都不知道自己想要什么，那么大学如何相信你会顺利完成学业？你的语气应该坚定、优雅，表示你对自己和学校有清楚的了解。注意，自信的语气也说明你没有在"求"学校录取你。

从语气中还能看出你的真实性。从很多同学的申请材料中能看出来自其他地方"声音"的痕迹。通常，这些学生不知道如何回答学校的问题，于是，他们就模仿、借鉴别人的申请材料。从这种拼凑在一起的文字里，可以一目了然看出申请人自己的声音是缺场的，说明他们不是有备而来的。这种情况下，学生很难被录取。还有一种情况是，申请人没有表现真实的自己。比如，你明明想学医学，但家长让你学金融，这样在申请金融院校时，你的语气就会暴露你的不诚实，因为对一件事情的激情是很难装出来的。

为什么你和你申请的专业是契合的？为什么你是该系的最佳人选，该系也是你的最佳去处？这是你应该自己考虑的问题。对自己的彻底了解可以让你知道自己能贡献什么。你的贡献是否也恰好是这所大学想要的？如果一所学校不够珍惜你的价值，那说明这所学校不适合你。感觉到被学校珍视说明你选对了地方。在北美，即使是同一个专业，在每所学校也是不一样的，因为每所学校都强调自己的特色，你必须从某种程度上对该校、该专业有所贡献。当你选对了学校、专业，你会感到满足、快乐、多产。

将自己跟学校配对并不等于说你就得迎合学校的喜好。时刻做真实的自己非常重要。即使你迎合了学校的各种条件，学校可能还是不会录取你。只要你对自己的内心忠诚，对自己的理想忠诚，你就一定不会错过对的专业、对的学校。

创造个人传奇

太多的中国学生在上大学前没有问过自己为什么要上大学。大家都觉得，上大学是自然而然的事情：高中以后必然要上大学，家长要求他们上大学，上完大学以后自然要找工作。还有人认为，拿学位是很光彩的事，这样别人就能看好自己，所以要上大学。事实上，因为没有很高的求学动机，学生容易在本科阶段由于竞争或者完不成学业而被淘汰。

接受高等教育的最终目的，是让教育把你推向你的个人使命和你所能创造的个人传奇（personal legend）。"个人传奇"这个概念最初来自巴西作家保罗·科艾略（Paulo Coelho）的寓言小说《炼金术士》（*The Alchemist*）。"个人传奇"主要是说，你希望自己如何被历史记住，如何被他人记住。如果历史将你的生平浓缩成一句话，那么，这句话应该是什么？拿到大学录取通知只是个开始。要让大学生活过得印象深刻而有意义，你需要常常把它与本书前两篇提出的问题联系在一起。至于如何定义自己，如何服务，有何价值，要给人类历史留下什么，这些问题都是你自己的故事。

至此，我知道，读到这里的你一定是不凡的，是快乐的，是成功的。

致　谢

感谢我父母对我一如既往的支持、帮助和爱。感谢所有我教过的学生，特别是 Steven Zhang，Shu Lu 给予本书的支持。感谢加拿大畅销书作家 Raymond Aaron 激发了我写这本书的灵感，也感谢加拿大运动员 Mark Mckoy 对本书的关注和支持。

Win in North America

—A Must-Have Book for Chinese Young Adults Who Study in North America

BY Can Zheng

Central Radio & TV University Press

Beijing

About the Author

Can Zheng studied modernism and received her Master of Arts from the University of Victoria. She was one of the contributors to *Global Literary Theory : An Anthology*.

Also by Can Zheng

Out of the Cocoon, Are You the Butterfly?
The Nest—Poems 2014
Sage

For My Parents

Contents

I. Self-Development

II. Self-Realization

III. Self-Training

I. Self-Development

Seminar 1

Cultural Differences between China and North America

No matter where you are from, you cannot excel in North American schools or universities without a thorough understanding of your individuality and life purpose. Once you have truly understood your mission, your potentials will unfold naturally, and you will feel exalted by where you are going. Potential is the infinite you—the real you beyond all your current understandings of yourself. Reaching toward your potentials seems to be a huge and intimidating project, but by guiding you to the roots of your soul, I will make the process easy.

The majority of Chinese students, like you, go to Canada or the United States to study. When English becomes your second language and you enroll in the North American education system, the cultural shifts and identity changes begin. Maybe you have already consciously or unconsciously noticed this phenomenon, but do not know how to deal with it. You may feel like a pendulum oscillating in between two

different ends. The confusion might exist for a while, but trust me—this process will nourish and grow you in many ways, until one day you establish a new North American identity based on truly valuing and acknowledging your Chinese roots.

Collectivism and Individualism

China has a time-honored history, which means its history can be dated back to thousands of years ago. On the contrary, North American countries are not ancient but relatively "young" at merely hundreds of years old. This by no means suggests that Chinese culture is superior to North American culture or vice versa. They have their own advantages and disadvantages. For example, Chinese culture has extensive wisdom that has been tested and practiced throughout time, whereas North American culture builds upon the rest of the world's cultural legacies and commits to new frontiers and innovative humanity.

What is collectivism? Like other Asian countries, collectivism is one of the most important characteristics of Chinese culture. Being collectivist means that each individual is not as important as the group a person belongs to. This requires each individual to be relatively similar to others, and

each one contributes to the wellbeing of the group. A group can be a family, a circle of friends, the community you work for, and so on. This creates a significant amount of co-dependency and cooperation among one another. One might feel uncomfortable or insecure once being isolated from the group.

Individualism does not solely belong to North America. It is a common feature of all English-speaking countries because it was derived from the root of Western cultures. Traditionally speaking, individualism emphasizes individual value and uniqueness, which significantly separates one individual from another. In collective cultures, one realizes one's value mainly through being one of the members of the group. Individualism, however, allows a person to realize his or her own values even if the group is absent.

As for Chinese students, many of you noticed this change when you first came to Canada or the United States. Some friends I know, even if they have already reached adulthood, still feel tremendously insecure when doing things alone. Going to school or going shopping with companions makes them a lot more comfortable. In other words, co-dependency will be severely challenged if you resist the changes of cultural identity. It does not mean you should forget about being Chinese and change into someone you are not. You can, of

course, choose whatever identity you wish, but building your own individualism is something you cannot escape from. The more you avoid it, the more it will stand in front of your face like a roadblock.

Commonness and Uniqueness

Although globalization, during the recent decades, is mingling collectivist and individual cultures together, in the past, collectivist culture asks each one to erase one's speciality. We may still experience this in our collective unconscious mind. Perhaps, as you grow up, parents' and schools' education tends to punish individualism so you can be "someone not too different." For example, you might have heard to "not be the first to speak up," "wait until others have finished," etc. By and by, when you are distinct, you might instantly fear the hidden judgement and criticism, or even isolation. Some parents push their children so they can excel in every area, but these children just want to be themselves and be ordinary. Being unique means you know why you are different and fully accept all your differences. You do not have to look or act like someone else.

There will not be another you, or another individual who

can replace your position in the world. In North America, the personal choice is relatively emphasized. Every one is encouraged to be absolutely different from the rest of society. As you came here, you experience a huge cultural shift. The primary thing you need to find out is your uniqueness, which might have been buried or repressed before. Discovering your uniqueness can help you recognize where your potentials might be, and help you lay the most important psychological foundation for your academic success. Once you are comfortable with your own uniqueness, your confidence will soar and you will feel completely OK with being individualistic. There is a saying that goes, " Be you, the world will adjust. "

Silence and Voice

Silence is not a negative word; on the contrary, it is tremendously powerful. Most Chinese students experienced criticism from teachers or peers, who complained about their muteness. Silence is conventionally regarded as "no ideas" in the North American academia. Despite the fact that the frontier of the North American culture is changing and starting to value silence, the academic world still maintains the

logocentric tradition, which means you have to speak up.

From my teaching experience, I found that Chinese students are "silent" for several reasons. First, you know the answer but you do not think it is necessary to speak it out instantly. Second, you know the answer but you are waiting for other students to speak first. Third, you know the answer but you do not think in words but pictures; the knowledge is latent and you cannot immediately translate the image into words. Many teachers who do not know how to teach Chinese students will simply give up or bluntly regard them as slow, which further hinders their improvement in, say, ENG3U/4U studies. Relating "silence" with lack of intelligence is just a type of ignorance. I trained Chinese students by changing their mental images or discrete ideas into words and logic. In doing so, teachers have to be patient listeners and trust that every student is intelligent. They just need more time (See "Self-Training" section).

Imagery and Logic

Another big difference Chinese students need to be aware of is how we think. Because the Chinese language was created in a totally different way, as the form of a Chinese character

pictures its meaning, Chinese people do not think strictly in linear logic. The English language, however, follows what Ferdinand de Saussure calls "arbitrariness." It means the form of a word has almost nothing to do with its meaning. Due to the imagery of Chinese language, Chinese students are good at studying English poetry, even if they find difficulties in learning about English drama and novels. The English language system is strictly grammatical and requires each sentence to be complete. This is why when Chinese students start to learn how to think and write in English, grammar becomes a big issue. Native English speakers have grammatical problems, too, but cognitively, they differ from Chinese students' grammatical barriers. The common problem Chinese students face is that the sentences are usually fragmented, and the passage does not have a linear logic flow. Instead, the "logic" is usually repetitive and reiterates the same thing over and over again, since the thoughts aim to describe the mental pictures.

I will give you some logic and academic writing trainings in the third part of the book. They will guide you to understand how to disentangle your mental images into linear logic. Please also remember that any good work requires tons of practice. The more academic writings you complete, the

better your logic will be. This training is supposed to be done before you enter the university. That is, you should master your linear logic and academic writing during, at least, the ENG3U and ENG4U period, so you can use logical thinking and academic writing as useful tools to do research and explore the world.

Seminar 2

Recognize Your Talents and Gifts

In North America, the self has to experience one or several transformations. Without strong and stable individualism, you may feel that your core is pulled in all sorts of directions. To establish your individualism, your first job is to figure out what unique talents and gifts you naturally have. No one in the world can possess your talents and gifts, not even your parents or siblings. For example, you are a music genius, but there are lots of music prodigies in the world. How can you be different from others? In his *The Seven Spiritual Laws of Success* (Chapter 9), Deepak Chopra expresses the idea that even if you have a similar talent to others, your expression of that talent must be totally unique. I understand "gift" as something you were born with, which means you do not have to be taught. Instead, you can teach others. Gifts and talents are similar; they compose your entire uniqueness.

Some students' parents asked me why they could not find

any talent in their children whatsoever. By talents and gifts, they do not necessarily mean something grand or glamorous. Not everyone can be Lady Gaga or Stephen Hawking, but every one is gifted in some way. For example, some students are naturally very tidy; they can organize their room extremely well. This might mean they could be gifted managers. Some students are hard to control; it is extremely difficult for them to obey something. They might become successful leaders in the future, like CEOs, bosses, etc. It is important for all the students and parents to bear in mind that talents and gifts can be something big or can be something "small." One is not superior to the other because everyone plays important roles in the world and everyone's talents and gifts matter for the evolvement of humanity.

Use Your Pain

The first technique for you to find out your talents and gifts is to use your pain. Perhaps you have lived a happy life so far. That is, you do not have any pain. In this case, you can skip this section and read from "Listen to Your Inner Voice" onward. This section is for students who have buried something huge inside. They feel somehow afflicted because

certain talents and gifts cannot be known by the world.

I always believe that, before you become who you really are, you are usually your opposite. I have a perfect example here. A student I coached a few months ago received admission from the University of Waterloo two hours after submitting the application. She is passionate about travelling; her dream is to see the world and this desire has to be combined with study and work simultaneously. When I was talking to her, I instantly discovered that this desire for travel was severely repressed because her family environment, either too strict or too overprotective (like many Chinese families) , does not allow her to leave home and travel. What is repressed in our sub-consciousness throughout time becomes accumulatively powerful and overt.

The pain exists for a reason: It is for you to recognize what you really want. Usually, what you want shows what you are good at. That is where your talents and gifts reside. For example, I know that one of my former students desires to be a superstar, but she feels depressed because her parents want her to go to another direction and her light thus cannot shine. Another former student I taught has a compassionate nature, but the outside environment requires him to be selfish and egotistic. The boy becomes silent and introverted. His eyes

start to shine when people really understand his humanitarian soul. These examples show that your pain, misery, and depression are good indicators which will point you toward your real desire, which is what you are good at. So, use what pains you and what aches you the most, and you can easily find out your talents and gifts. Once you find the true passion, it will stay with you forever. This is why some scientists persist in working in labs everyday into their 80s, some entrepreneurs still do public speaking when they are 70, and some musicians cannot stop creating songs as long as they are alive.

Listen to Your Inner Voice

Another case is that some students are multi-passionate (like me). They have too many talents and gifts and too many interests, so it is confusing for them to know what they are good at or what they want. Knowing who you are is a journey or a process. You have to spend enough time exploring yourself fully. Be patient.

Here I give you the second tip—listen to your inner voice that emerges repeatedly and find out what you are really good at. When I was six or seven, I was obsessed with piano. My parents bought me a piano and I enjoyed the lesson for a few

years. Later it dawned on me that I was not really good at playing this instrument. Voices from other sources let me know that I should continue learning it, but the inner voice strongly told me that I should give up. This is because I had other important things to do. Actually, the inner voice repeatedly whispered that I should be a writer. That voice has lasted for years, which means its authenticity was tested throughout time, so the inner voice should be trusted.

If you feel overwhelmed, confused, or even exhausted because you have too many talents to develop, you should trust your inner voice and figure out which talents are authentic and which are just transient or vain. When you become a good listener to your inner voice, you will realize which gift has its priority and you will expend more time and energy on that. I am not saying you should only have one gift—it can be multiple. Instead, you have to prioritize them and pay attention to their value so you can eventually see achievements in those areas.

Let Your Joy Guide You

If, after applying the previous two tips, you still cannot find your talents and gifts, or secretly believe you do not have

any, then the third tip might work for you. The key is to let joy guide you. This is a popular notion that every success coach must talk about. Especially in North America, this principle is pervasive enough to be common sense. What does joy mean? For me, it means a deeper sense of excitement, exaltation and satisfaction for doing something. When you are doing this "something," you cannot feel time. Nothing from the outside environment can distract you from your work. Then, you can also find your talents and gifts through locating these feelings.

Following your joy differs from following your interests. Letting your interests guide you can be misleading. Your interests may originate from your admiration of some superstars, other friends' influence and so forth, especially when you are a teenager (your characters are still developing). For example, you are interested in Rock and Roll, but later you realize the band you started has not gone anywhere. For another example, you are interested in manicure and spend lots of time on studying it, because all the girls are doing it fantastically. Later you realize you just picked up others' interests. You just did some fun things to kill time or unconsciously avoid being bored. Those things, however, are not the real you, nor your real talents and gifts.

If you let joy guide you, you will not feel bored or

limited. Instead, you feel 1) exalted and expanded; 2) your potential is unfolding in an unlimited way; 3) you work hard but seldom feel tired; 4) you seldom care about the result of your effort. For example, some students love philosophies and theories. They are excited about expanding their mind. A two-hour class for them is like twenty minutes. For another example, some students enjoy being on stage. Under the spotlight makes them feel as if time stops forever. Some students love communication. When talking to others, they can talk endlessly without feeling tired. Remember that the word "joy" is almost ineffable. It is a deeper sense of acknowledgement of your unique existence. From now on, you can start to consciously locate where your "joy" is. If you develop a habit of letting joy guide you, clarity will gradually show up for you.

Honor Your Chinese Blood

The Chinese descent is something latent yet extremely powerful. Coming to Canada has made me more Chinese than before, for I really notice the value of the blood that has been passed on from generation to generation. This becomes my asset or what I am truly proud of. Therefore, another shortcut

to find out your talents and gifts is to study a little bit about your family history. What are the dreams and passions and talents of your parents or your grandparents? Are there any dreams that were repressed in the past? Are there any unfulfilled desires? Do all the family members share some similar talents? These explorations might inspire you. I do not mean that you let your parents and grandparents define you. For example, just because all your relatives are doctors, does not mean you must be good at curing people. Who you are is your own choice, but knowing your family history can give you many insights.

Take myself as an example. I grew up in a family of teachers. Actually, they have been teachers for four generations (I am the fifth generation). Being a teacher was just so natural for me. However, if I truly honor my blood, I not only want larger "classrooms," but I also want to expand the scope of traditional teaching. I want more people to be inspired. This acknowledgement led me to writing nonfictions, novels and poetry. In this way, I can continue honoring my blood (the family tradition), and at the same time creatively expand the family legend. The opposite might also be true. For example, everyone in your family is an engineer. You deeply rebel against this tradition, and believe you are

someone different. Say, you want to be a musician. The reverse way matters as well.

The key is to honor the history that accumulates in your blood as intangible treasures. Remember that every tradition is at the same time something TIMELESS. It has the vitality to be renewed again and again. This is also the advantage of North American culture; it is built upon the traditions of the rest of the world. For any North American individual, understanding your roots can empower you significantly. I think, for all Chinese students, when you start to honor what has been established and accomplished in your past, you can figure out and acknowledge the genius in you.

Seminar 3

Find Your Life Purpose

If you have talents and gifts but do not use them to benefit humanity, they could be wasted. This is also the deepest root of unhappiness. Perhaps you do not know what your life purpose is. Finding it as early as you can is one of the keys to your academic success. A clear purpose will make you become goal-oriented. Once your goals are specific, success will become much easier. I am lucky in this respect because my life purpose came to me early. The life purpose is the answer to the questions, "Why are you here?" "What are you here to do?" and "How can you realize the value of your life?" Life purpose might be revealed to you early in your childhood or teenage years as a dream. As you grow up, how to realize that dream will become more and more specific. For example, you might dream of becoming a superstar in your childhood. Later you realize that being a leading scientist is the way to realize it.

Life purpose goes much deeper to the core meaning of your being. It is, therefore, different from your talents and gifts, yet the first two seminars have laid crucial foundations for the understanding of the third one. Your life purpose brings you the ultimate passion for overcoming any type of difficulties you may encounter in your academic life. Most Chinese students who are currently studying in North America grew up in prosperous families. I believe you seldom have to worry about hunger, homelessness, and material scarcity. Being materially well-provided for allows you to focus on "higher needs." According to psychologist Abraham Maslow's "hierarchy of needs," the highest three needs are the need for love/belongingness, the need for self-esteem, and the need for self-realization[①]. In North America, most people spend their lifetimes chasing these three needs, especially the last one. Entering into this cultural milieu somehow forces you, sooner or later, to figure out the answers to these questions. If you can consciously seek your life purpose, the answer will come to you. Otherwise, your academic life might be severely affected. The most commonly seen consequence is that many Chinese students hate their majors; they waste their parents'

---

①黄希庭：《人格心理学》，378 页，杭州，浙江教育出版社，2002。

money and cannot graduate on time. Wherever you are right now, either in Canadian/American high schools or universities, the following questions will help you clarify your life purpose, which will in every way push you toward academic success.

Why Are You Here on Earth?

Each one of us came to life for a specific purpose—this is why life is by no means meaningless. Reincarnation only happens when there is a purpose to fulfill. The entire journey of one's life is to move toward that destination. You may have heard that some people suffer from depression or other dysfunctions in their lives. The absence of happiness can only occur when one's life purpose is not fulfilled. Each one has a life purpose that differs from anyone else's. It does not mean that one is more valuable than the other. People are equal because they have equal values on earth. The world needs all kinds of people to fulfill all kinds of purposes.

I am not too worried about talking about such " big " questions to Chinese teenagers and young adults. On the contrary, the younger you are, the easier you can find why you are here on Earth. The world's cultures are integrating so quickly and becoming more and more homogenous. It is

common nowadays for you to experience personal awakening or enlightenment. In fact, many of my former students have already found the answer. They were determined, and I knew they would definitely achieve their life mission.

From the previous seminars, we know that talents and gifts are what you naturally have; somehow you do not have to "learn" them. Yet life purpose asks you to USE your gifts and talents to BENEFIT the rest of the world. The focus shifts from "you" to the RELATIONSHIPS between "you" and "others." For example, you are good at reconciling conflicts between your parents; you crave peace and harmony. This gift might be used, not only for your parents, but bringing justice and peace to the world. You might become a brilliant judge, a counsellor, and so forth. If you are generous with money, then being a philanthropist could be your path. The key is to think about how you can SERVE the world by using your gifts and talents. Then let the answer naturally come to you.

Who Are You Indeed?

This is the question that always appears in our minds. If your confidence constantly fluctuates like a roller coaster, you probably do not know who you really are. Your confidence

23

may soar if you get an A, but drop instantly when you get a C. Many adults identify themselves with their titles, as Deepak Chopra suggests in his *The Seven Spiritual Laws of Success* (Chapter 2). Once the title of "president" or "professor" is gone, the self-esteem suffers tremendously. Similarly, if you let your awesome girlfriend or your rich parents define you, then your self-confidence will be at stake sooner or later. Once one's true self is found, a person's confidence will not go up and down, but always be stable. If you get a C, for example, a real confident person will not relate it to the unworthiness of the self. Instead, C only suggests that something needs to be improved and it will propel you to an A——this is the voice of the authentic self.

One's identity changes over time, but what really defines one's core, the value of being, the true self that stabilizes your confidence, is your life purpose. I partly agree with Deepak Chopra that "who we are" has two components: 1) you are unique because you have been given certain special talents and gifts. This is why you were created to be a human being; 2) you serve humanity with your talents and gifts (see *The Seven Spiritual Laws of Success*, Chapter 9). For example, your cultural identity may shift from Chinese to Chinese American and then back to Chinese again, but your life purpose is relatively stable. You are a talented dancer, and your life

purpose is to inspire people through the beauty of dancing. Thus, wherever you go, you can still serve humanity in a certain way regardless of the cultural boundaries. As long as you are using the talents to SERVE others, you are the true self.

The irony is that "who you are" is not a self-centered question: You cannot consider this question without thinking about others. Thus the true self is actually selfless, which is the opposite of egotism. Our personal value is realized only through helping others. Otherwise, no matter how gifted you are, the gift would lose its meaning and value.

How Can You Achieve It in This Lifetime?

Life purpose, once you find it, looks so huge and idealistic. You have to break it down and make it practical. For example, I found my purpose years ago, which is to improve the modern culture. It came to me like an epiphany. Gradually, the path to achieve it becomes clear. I became obsessed with all kinds of theories and literature. Reading turned out to be a habit, and knowledge becomes my strength. As I was about to finish my master's degree, I received training from Jack Canfield, the most influential success coach in the United States. In a meditation, I saw that the symbol of my life

purpose was a book, so I realized that writing is the practical way to have my purpose manifested into reality. What you do every day embodies your life purpose so that something intangible becomes tangible. If you feel it is so grand and remote, and therefore you can never achieve it, then you need to make it into the content of your everyday life.

For high school and university students, volunteering is a great way for you to find and implement a life purpose. The value of volunteering lay in the fact that it asks you whether you feel happy about serving others for free. Many Chinese students, once they start to do volunteer work, will gradually fall in love with serving others without expecting some material benefits. I have asked many students, no matter how rich their families are, and they all love volunteering in the end because the joy and the inner fulfillment are priceless.

Once your life purpose is clear to you, all sorts of opportunities will show up. Other than volunteering, you can seize the chance to deliver a speech, give a performance, meet new people, join a competition, go to an event, and so on. All your social activities will gradually become focused and meaningful. On top of that, you will have lots of joy. This is how you can ground your life purpose, which seems so abstract, into reality.

How Can Life Purpose Benefit Your Study?

As high school and university students, finding your life purpose essentially benefits your academic studies. This is indeed the ultimate way to unlock your highest potential. Education in North America is here to help you unfold your dreams rather than "educate" you by putting knowledge into your brains. North American education (especially university education) provides a nourishing soil for all your potentials to flourish—so use it well.

Before entering into the university, you had better already be clear about your life purpose. A student I taught had grown up in a wealthy family, but she suffered from asthma when she was little. Those doctors who took care of her touched her so deeply that she wanted to be someone like them. Her personal mission is to save children's lives. She was not doing well in her studies when I met her, but as I helped her exteriorize her personal mission, I felt that a light was turned on. She did not regard study as a pressure any more. Instead, she has the eagerness to learn because she can see the big picture. Thus, university will serve your purpose—it is not somewhere we have to go but somewhere we want to go.

Changing your attitude from being reactive to proactive, with the assistance of a clear life purpose, is key to making the most of a university education. The majority of Chinese students I taught before were getting used to being "taught." Waiting for knowledge to come into your brain is not a good way to learn because your mind is passive and reactive. Being proactive means you have already studied ahead and come up with plenty of questions and actively expect answers to come. In this way, you can shine wherever you go. Traditional Chinese culture may require you to hide your genius, but North American culture asks you to shine your genius out. The benefit is huge, and you will feel happier and more fulfilled.

II. Self-Realization

Seminar 4

Maximize Your Potentials

What does potential actually mean? For me, it means the limitlessness in you that has yet to be discovered. Quantum physicist Dr. John Hagelin told us in the movie "The Secret" that "we are using only 5% of the human mind and only 1% is the result of proper education." Schools and universities can push us forward, either negatively or positively, yet how to maximize your potential is your own job. It is the skill you must master as early as possible.

To maximize your potential, we first need to understand how our mind works. Our consciousness thinks through words. Whether you think in Chinese or English, as long as you think in the form of words, your conscious mind is working. The unconscious mind is different (Note: I am not talking about the subconscious) ; it thinks through images, like a movie without words. When you are falling asleep, the conscious mind gradually stops and the unconscious mind starts to work.

Are dreams not images, movements, and symbols all the time? Both consciousness and unconsciousness have tremendous amounts of power; both of them can help you achieve your goals. Knowing how to use your words and mental images (affirmation and visualization) is a major tool to open your mental power.

Clarify What You Want

Clarifying what you really want is a prerequisite: You cannot achieve anything without having at least one goal in mind. Usually we do not ask for what we really want, because the glamour of success actually intimidates us. "What if I really get an A?" "What if I really got into Yale?" "What if all my classmates give me a round of applause and I have to blush?" Success might feel uncomfortable because you have to stretch yourself so much in order to achieve it. The opposite is true, too. You might often be afraid of getting a C, or afraid of being judged by your teachers. Maybe you do not want to end up being isolated from other kids. What you do not want is a "want" as well because the unconscious mind does not think in logic. Whatever mental picture you have in mind is a "want."

True desire is free from the above chaos. First, think about if you are holding yourself back because what you want is too big. I would encourage you to be audacious and bold. For example, you want to be a movie star, but you hide it and think a degree in science is not too bad, either. You might desire to be a great musician, but your parents ask you to be an architect. You actually end up wanting what your parents want. So, to identify what you really want is to examine if you are totally honest with yourself. Second, look at the opposite of your fears. If you are afraid of eating lunch alone at school, what you really want is to have loving friends who can be with you at lunch. If you are afraid of doing a presentation, what you really want is to be a good public speaker. If you are afraid that you cannot get the degree, what you really want is to successfully graduate. By looking at the other side of your hidden fears, you can easily identify your true desires. Removing fake and negative desires is, therefore, a quick way to approach clarity.

Making your desires super clear means you have already opened the door to success. In quantum physics, the infinite possibilities in space change according to the intention we put out. Clarifying what you want saves you plenty of time because you can focus all your energies on your goal and thus move

toward it faster. This is the first step to maximizing your potential.

10% Visualization and Affirmation

Once your goal is clear, you may feel excited for a moment and might quickly forget about it! It is fine—I understand that. Most people cannot realize their dreams because they give up too soon. Their potentials, accordingly, cannot be properly developed. It is important to constantly remind yourself of what you want. Two practical techniques are visualization and affirmation. These are the methods of using your unconscious and conscious mind so your potentials are expanded.

Visualization is to present your goal with a picture or a symbol, which is a snapshot of your goal when it is achieved. Our visions are powerful because our unconscious mind holds a tremendous amount of hidden power that can be infinitely developed. For example, what you really want is to receive an offer from the University of Toronto. Then you can change your laptop wallpaper into a campus picture. If you have stayed in a university for seven years and really want to graduate, you can put a graduation ceremony image in front of

you and take it as your own big moment! When the unconscious mind "digests" the image that represents your true desire, it will move toward it for sure.

Affirmation is using your conscious mind to propel you toward what you want. Your inner voice embodies the power of your conscious mind. If you are nervous in class and think, "Oh, the teacher will call my name," then your name will be called. If you think, "My mom will criticize me for not getting a degree," then you will be criticized. Learning how to replace your negative language into a positive one can boost your energy level and attract victories. When you say affirmations, remember to change your future tense into present tense, present perfect or past tense. I discovered that the past tense affirmation is the most powerful because it convinces your mind that something has already been achieved. For example, I saw that some students were struggling with not being able to graduate on time. You can simply say to yourself, "I have already graduated." It is more powerful than, "I want to graduate," or, "I will graduate." "I will be an A student" is less powerful than "I am an A student." Affirmation is not positive attitude, but affirms what you believe and erases the illusion of time.

90% Take Action

We have already talked about clarifying what you want and the power of the mind. This is just 10% of the entire game. 90% of the time should be spent on taking action. You cannot say "I am an A student" but then act like a C student. You cannot say, "I successfully received my degree" but then fail to do your homework. Actions tell your brain that you are serious. For example, when you frequently say, "I am an A student," you by and by feel that you are intelligent, you WANT to work hard, and you study late at night without feeling exhausted. You often have to do something to tell yourself that you actually mean it. For example, you seldom speak up during class, but one day you suddenly raise your hand to prove that you are the best student. The reason is that you have perceived yourself in this way already. Your actions have to match your intention, your visualization and affirmation.

Action is not something escapable; every successful person takes MASSIVE amounts of action and spends time on visualization and affirmation only when necessary. If you gradually notice that you are productive and have nearly neglected your visions and affirmative words, this is a good sign that your success is now tangible. Chances are you will

soon get the result you want. For example, you have visualized about graduation and fed your brain with affirmative thoughts. Days later you realize you care nothing about graduation but focus all your attention on your writing your thesis in the library. This is because action taking fuels you up. Other distractions do not have a chance to squeeze into your occupied mind at all. As you have finally achieved your goal (say, you hold the degree in your hands) , success feels tangible and real. Most importantly, you deserve it.

Encourage and Reward Yourself

Celebrating every achievement is a huge encouragement for further victories. Even if the achievement is so small— say, you just raised your hand to answer a question for the first time—it is worth celebrating. You can ask your family and friends to celebrate your progress with you. If they are not available, you can reward yourself all the same. For example, if you want to buy something, buy it after your achievement. If you want to see a movie, do it after you get an A. Every step you make is marvellous. The more you reward your achievement, the more accomplishments there will be for you to celebrate.

Parents are great helpers in this respect. You can ask

your parents to work with you. For example, ask your mother to only buy that book you love when you have finished composing a music piece. It is also extremely important to ask them to encourage you if you did not achieve it. People who are close to you are like a team. Their feedback can monitor your improvement in an effective way. My parents helped me enormously. I let them know immediately after achieving something because I wanted to hear positive words. I get better whenever they say, "I am proud of you." By and by, I established a self-rewarding system with my parents. Not only does it work well, but also our relationship has constantly improved.

You can select several good friends as accountability partners, too. Make sure they are 100% supportive and positive. Whatever you achieve, even if you fail, they will be there for you! In return, you can be your friends' accountability partner. Truly supportive friends will not send you judgement, criticism, or jealousy. You grow up together like a team. You can go to movies together after achieving a certain goal. You can throw a party or make a film together, etc. Rewarding your effort enlightens your soul. Consequently, you want to accomplish more, and you get valuable friendships in return.

Seminar 5

Be Competitive without Competing

You might have noticed that, after coming to North America, competition becomes different and severe. The best form of competition that always let you win is, ironically, "not to compete with others." This works all the time for me. I somehow understand this because I am familiar with ancient Chinese philosophies, especially Daoism. Dao convinces me that the most invincible warrior does not compete with others. I have shown you the secrets that can make you competitive in the previous seminars. This seminar tells you how to deal with competition since your invincibility has already caught lots of attention.

To excel in any kind of competition is to learn from failures, be the authentic you, ignore what others are doing and run your own race. If you always focus on being who you are, you will not compare yourself with others, feel jealous, or be easily distracted. Instead, you only concentrate on what you

are here to offer, and you always win respect and admiration.

You Were Born to Win

I deeply believe that everyone was born to win in this lifetime, regardless of how much you have been through. On the contrary, the more failures you had before, the more likely you will rise up to the top. Any type of difficulty nourishes you, and the lessons you have learned make you stronger and more capable. When I was in elementary school, I had some learning difficulties. My maths was horribly bad, and my Grade 2 teacher used to tell my parents that my logic was "weird." Despite all the learning difficulties and all the symptoms that made me look autistic, my left-brain intelligence slowly evolved. However, I appreciate all that experience. What happened later was that I read massively and extensively, and not only did my logic develop, but I received my MA degree in English literature. Whatever you are struggling with in your studies, the effort will be paid off because you are destined to win. Tell yourself that "failure" does not exist in your life. The current difficulty is just there to help you grow.

If you are facing any kind of competition, you should

study yourself well and find a niche. In this world of endless possibilities, there must be some niche that has not been filled yet, and that niche must WANT your talents and gifts. The best way for competition is that you find a way to express your uniqueness. Like I said in the previous seminars, use your talents and gifts well. And because you are so unique that no one else in the world can replace you, you become naturally competitive. In other words, there is something that only you can do, so nobody can surpass you. In this way, only YOU are YOUR competitor. You compare everyday with yourself, and improvement is your own growth.

Be Audacious and Friendly

Competition may sound cruel and annoying, but I do not feel that way. If you try to avoid competition, it will ironically find you again and again. You want to develop a fighter's mentality to always embrace challenges, and learn how to fight a good fight. During competition, the best winners are bold enough to say yes to the challenge before they actually know how to do it. A Chinese student I met had not read English literature, for she felt that it was so intimidating to read a whole book in English. It is common logic that we refuse to

take challenge because we do not know how to do something, but a highly competitive person will say yes and then figure out how to do it. Most of the time, the biggest enemy is that thing in between your two ears. If you want to be a winner, you need to be audacious in front of the difficult things and the unknown.

The really competitive individuals do not look intimidating at all. Rather, they have balanced self-esteem and are friendly. Sometimes competition becomes so intense that it is actually a battle of ego. Other people may make you look vulnerable, or bring you down so they can rise up higher. When you are talented, people may be jealous. They want to bring you down to their level so you cannot win. To be a real winner, you should avoid wasting your energy thinking about how other people feel about you. You need to master the skills of focusing on running your own race and enjoying your own time. Those who are jealous and constantly bringing you down are not smart enough, because they do not spend energy on developing their own skills. This is why you excel.

Never Put out Negativity

The positive energy you give to the world will always

come back. If you want to win, then encourage other people to win. For example, girls in school gossip about you, but you cannot gossip about them in return. This is not a good energy flow, and the consequence is that none of you can win. The competitive people always win because, wherever they go, they give positive energy and lighten people up. The same energy comes back to them. Smart people know that the more positivity they give to the world, the more light they own.

To be competitive, you need to skilfully and consciously protect your energy space and weed out possible negativity. Meanwhile, you also work hard on not giving negative energies out to the world. Thus you become invincible without competing with others, for nothing can hurt your winner's aura. By and by, because you hold lots of positive energy, you attract more support and applause from the world. Whatever jealousy or animosity that tries to tear you down is destined to fail.

Be Calm and Receive Victory

Chinese culture may ask you to be humble, but North American culture most likely requires you to be comfortable with receiving compliments, thank-you speeches, and so forth. I am not saying you are not your Chinese self any more. Be

proud of your CHINESE ROOTS that made you and nourished you, but also be proud of the new you and receive victory wherever you go.

You cannot be a winner by constantly hiding yourself—let people know! Modesty and confidence are not self-contradictory. All the strengths and self-esteem come from knowing who you are and being who you are. Some Chinese students are shy and introverted. I was an introvert as well, but I gradually realized that hiding myself is not working for me. North American culture does not really get the irony that if you are introverted, you must be somebody. What I want to say is that you need to develop a habit of receiving all kinds of successes with ease. This will enhance your aura. Deep inside, becoming a good receiver means you value your personal contribution to the world. It is a deeper acknowledgement that makes you feel that you deserve compliments or rewards.

Seminar 6

Win in Hard Times

Chinese parents are usually overprotective, but it does not prevent their children from undergoing sufferings. The difficulties will come for everyone—this is normal not because you have sudden bad luck but because you have a future in front of you. If you are battling with difficult situations, like depression, a loss, a broken heart, and so forth, please understand that everything difficult happens for a reason. The hardships are here to help you grow so you can become better.

How you act in difficult times proves who you are. Everyone's life has some misfortunes, but different reactions separate people. Maybe you have worked hard but still received a C on your test. Maybe you have trained for months but still failed that game. Maybe you loved your girlfriend so much, but she still left you. These are common. A positive attitude will turn dirt into gold. A true winner wins under good circumstances and bad, because a true winner sees the hidden

blessing beneath the misfortune and grasps every opportunity to rise to the top.

Focus on Your Faith

By faith I mean something you believe in. For example, you believe you are smart. It does not have to be something grand. In hard times, faith is challenged and tested. For example, you did not do well on a quiz—the mark was astonishingly low. You started to question whether you are still the best student in the class. This self-doubt is completely natural. Yet, faithful young people know how to turn this around. You can simply turn fear—" I'm not the best anymore"—into, "The quiz is here to tell me how to improve, and it helps me become even better. " When the odds are against you, true winners spend energy expanding their faith.

Fear is the expectation of failure. Fear usually arises because you do not know much about it. Lack of a proper amount of knowledge may make you feel at stake. Nobody is afraid of things they are familiar with. For example, a chef is not afraid of cooking. A teacher is not afraid of public speaking. My trick to overcome any fear is to master the knowledge. Of course you have to put faith forward, but

working hard to possess the knowledge will eliminate fear thoroughly. Thereafter when you face similar situations, you remain cool, for you know how to handle it.

The Larger Picture

There are small difficulties, which will pass a few days later. There might also be severe afflictions you have to struggle with for a long time. It is not due to fear but somehow you cannot see hope or any possible light. For example, it is hard to find a real friend at school, so you feel like a wallflower. Perhaps you feel a childhood trauma is still lingering and restricting you. When this happens, you can still back up again and win in the end. The key is to focus on the larger picture, not on your current situation. By "larger picture" I mean the blueprint of your life that is pictured on the basis of your life purpose. Constantly reminding you of where you are heading to gives you incredible strengths to overcome the current challenges.

The darkest time is usually followed by the brightest time. If you cannot see the light, it means that the light is ahead of you. For example, when J. K. Rowling was writing the *Harry Potter* series, her life was difficult, but she focused

on the larger picture in her mind and wrote the stories that meant the most to her. When life hits the darkest places, as long as you constantly reminded yourself of what you will accomplish in this life, the difficulty will look trivial. When it is over, you will realize that all the hardships pushed you toward your dreams. They are helpful rather than disastrous.

Be Happy about the Stretch

You can choose to let difficulties defeat you or promote you. Smart students with a winner's mindset always feel excited about the stretch; they know they cannot grow quickly without being stretched from "level 1" to "level 10." The stretch feels like this: "It is impossible for me to do this." All undergraduate students feel a big stretch during the first term in university. They feel that the workload is insane. One month later they realize they just slept four to five hours per day. Chinese students find it especially hard if they did not establish a solid foundation in their English language learning in high school. When I was in graduate school, I had to sometimes read seven to eight books per day. My typical attitude was that "the impossible for me is possible." When you feel excited about conquering the impossible, the victory

is even more exciting. My reading ability grew dramatically when I thought I could manage the workload.

If you do not feel the stretch, then you are probably not growing significantly. As we have discussed in the previous seminars, you have found what should be developed; the university is the place for you to develop them all. Stretching all your ability, like stretching your muscles, is the training process. Some students can hardly change; they would like to stay in their comfort zone. Yet resisting the stretch cannot help you whatsoever. I saw that some Chinese students, when newly entering the university, avoided heavy workloads and went back to pursuing their pleasures. At the end of the first term, they had to drop three courses. When you face the workload, you had better fill your mind with a winner's attitude and be happy about the fact that your abilities are getting stretched.

Be Your Own Mentor

We all need several mentors in our lives, but usually they can only inspire us temporarily or in a specific field. The person who can mentor you forever is YOU. To mentor yourself, you need to read a lot. When I entered the University of Victoria, the library wowed me. The entire third floor was

filled with books on humanities. When I started to do my research, I gradually realized that the library was not enough. Thus, I had to borrow many books from libraries across North America. Weirdly, many interesting things I wanted to read about were not included in the library; they were either too new or not so "academic." My hungry brain constantly needed to be fed. The resources I used included libraries, audiobooks, eBooks, databases, blogs, encyclopaedias, and so forth. Reading extensively from all sorts of resources means you can find a good way to mentor yourself.

Secondly, you should be confident enough to know that professors and teachers do not know everything. Usually because their research limits their own minds, their scope could be narrower than yours. In other words, professors are experts in their own field, but they are not experts on everything. I realize that Chinese students tend to rely too much on the teachers and professors' knowledge so they do not have a chance to develop independent thinking and research. If you feel that professors do not know what you know, then you have probably found your own research field. This is why constantly being your own mentor is so important. You need not depend on the authorities. You can have your own voice.

Thirdly, you may one day find, after learning a lot, that

university itself is limited; it satisfies you no more. If this happens, you should also trust your own intuition and further mentor yourself in order to develop new skills and open new grounds. Probably as genius as you are, no education can truly "educate" you. University just pushed you toward where you should be. I think all the super successful people know this; they have to be their best mentor in the world. And it is free.

III. Self-Training

Training 1

Master Critical Thinking

Critical thinking is a tool that you can use in thinking, writing and reading. There are several stages of critical thinking. Notably, critical thinking is often misunderstood and misused. If we are not careful, it might become the birthplace of negativity. Therefore, it is important for us to know how to use it with control. When you truly master critical thinking, you will know that the highest form of critique is actually creation.

Critical Thinking for Beginners

As Chinese students move from ESL to academic English learning, critical thinking becomes more and more like a roadblock for them. It takes time to master critical thinking; it is true for all high school students from all ethnicities.

Critical thinking is to recognize problems like logical

Hence, critical thinking is not to criticize others or resort to cynicism. It aims at improving ideas, and making our ideas valuable and our mind productive. Critical thinking also aims at finding good points; thus it should not be negative, but constructive and creative.

To master your critical thinking does not mean your right brain is all of a sudden useless. Rather, your right brain can be the most important helper to the processing of your linear logic. In terms of how fast you can think, your imagination or inspirations come much faster than your logic. It takes a little time for logic to get from A to Z, but for right brainers, getting from A to Z happens instantly. For example, when you have to write an essay, the idea may enter your brain in a flash, but to prove it is time-consuming because you have make sure that every piece of evidence is right and every argument makes sense. The brilliance about the right brain is that immediate inspirations, insights, intuitions, epiphanies—however you name them—are always more accurate. Logic can make the judgement wrong, ironically. This is why we often experience that the instant knowing is proven to be true later. Therefore, as you are improving your critical thinking abilities, the right brain can be a great guidance for you, which points you in the right direction.

Do Not Develop a "Critical Spirit"

Too much critical thinking can make people more and more negative because the brain is trained to locate flaws. I have seen extremely negative people who are doing extremely well in their academic fields. Yet this is certainly not the energy I want because I do not want to have a critical spirit. In graduate school, I discovered an interesting research that makes a lot sense to me. In Ramsés Fuenmayor's article "Systems Thinking and Critique. I. What is critique?" he summarizes three types of critiques[1]. They are dogmatic critique, immanent critique, and transcendental critique, which are derived throughout the evolvement of western philosophy. It sounds esoteric, but let me put it simply: Dogmatic critique is the starting point, the baby step of critical thinking. It sounds like this: "I say this is right, and then it is right." Immanent critique is where, I find, "negativity" happens, where opposing sides deny each other back and forth endlessly. The highest level of critical thinking is called

---

[1]Fuenmayor, Ramsés. "Systems Thinking and Critique. I. What is Critique?" *Systemic Practice and Action Research*, 3. 6 (1990): 524-44. *SpringerLink*.

"transcendental critique," which is ultimately creative.

Most importantly, the mature critical thinking should not be negative or cynical, but creative and constructive. If you feel that your critical thinking ability significantly improves, but in the meantime you are more critical of yourself and others, then it means that the critical thinking has to be further developed. At the level of transcendental critique, the thinkers expand the scope of previous knowledge without actually spending energies denying it. It is to say, "There is something more," instead of, "You are not right." Usually, a great critical thinker also has a non-critical spirit. Authentic critical thinking positively creates valuable thoughts to the world.

Training 2

Master Academic Writing

Since high school, academic writing has been one of the crucial skills you must master, or else you cannot excel in university. Academic writing includes your comparative essays, persuasive essays, IELTS writing task 2, and basically all the essays you are going to write in your first university year. However, academic writing has some fixed patterns and is easy to grasp. For example, the purpose of this type of essay is usually to convince your readers about your main idea, and the main idea is your argument. The style is formal and academic; generally you are not supposed to write in colloquial English. How well you structure your essay indicates the strength of your logic flow.

Basic Structure and Linear Logic

The basic structure of academic writing consists of an

introduction, several body paragraphs and a conclusion. We all know that the first paragraph is introduction. Its core, no matter how long, is your thesis statement and how you will prove it. The length of the introduction varies according to the entire length of your paper. You have already known this, but what you might not know is that the introduction can be the last thing you write. The starting point of your logic/research is practically your evidence/examples, from which we develop the topic sentence of each body paragraph. From a system of body paragraphs, you get your conclusion. And then you come up with a thesis and write it in the introduction. The longer your essay is, the more likely you write the introduction last.

The structure of each body paragraph consists of a topic sentence, evidence/examples, the explanation of your evidence/examples, and a concluding sentence. What students often neglect is to explain your evidence/examples. After using evidence/examples to support your topic sentence, you cannot expect them to be self-evident to your readers. Another common mistake is that a body paragraph ends without a conclusion. Maybe you feel that conclusion is simply a repetition of a topic sentence. Or you feel the conclusion is not important. The consequence is that your paragraph is incomplete or looks unfinished without a concluding sentence.

My former students often complain that they do not know

how to write a conclusion. The function of any conclusion, either a conclusion of a paragraph or a conclusion of the whole essay, focuses on answering one question, and that is, "So what?" It pushes you to think about why you have to spend time arguing all the above. It is not a simple repetition of your introduction. Instead, a conclusion is more profound and thorough. A conclusion is also the best way to test whether or not you have made a clear logical argument. If you cannot come up with a conclusion, chances are your previous argumentation is messy. On the contrary, if you can naturally produce a conclusion, it indicates the previous argumentation is valid. Another commonly made mistake is to introduce new ideas or new information in your conclusion, which suggests that your essay is unfinished; the linear logic has to go on.

Linear logic is easy to master. If you write a sentence (let's mark it A), the following sentence (B) is supposed to expand the key information in sentence (A). Likewise, sentence (C) should develop the key information in sentence (B), until the concluding sentence closes the entire paragraph without offering further new information. Lack of logic usually indicates that the argumentation is repetitive, as if a complex of information is not entangled. Let's look at an example (excerpted from one of my drafts),

1) Rather than creating mysteriousness or ambiguity, it is these contradictions of his personality that disclose his unresolved Oedipus complex (A), the ongoing libidinal power of which drives him to seek for an ideal father (B). For fatherless Coriolanus (C), Menenius does not fit for the position of the father (D)...

Linear logic in the above paragraph is a chain of information that develops one after another. In sentence (A), the most important information is " contradictions of his personality," which explains "mysteriousness or ambiguity. " The second key information in sentence (A) is "unresolved Oedipus complex," which is further developed by " the ongoing libidinal power" in sentence (B). (B) ends with "an ideal father," so the next sentence must talk about "an ideal father. " Sentence (D) introduces new information "Menenius" the name, so the following sentence must explain "Menenius" is not a father. You see, linear logic is this simple.

Let's examine how linear logic is disrupted (ignore the grammatical mistakes),

2) The speaker of "The Road Not Taken" thinks that the two roads appear in front of him are the difficult choices

or changes in people's lives (A). I also find that it seems like both poems are to describe different views in different seasons (B). (Anonymous)

This often happens: The writer's thoughts jump too quickly from (A) to (B). However, (A) and (B) are not closely related. The key information in sentence A is "two roads," "difficult choices," and "changes in people's lives." The following sentence should develop what "difficult choices" are and then what "changes in people's lives" refers to. Instead of explaining what has been introduced in sentence A, the writer introduced new ideas further in sentence (B), which are "different views" and "different seasons." Thus there is a logical gap in between (A) and (B). If (B) should continue, we can guess the next sentence should talk about what "both poems" are, and then "views" and "seasons." When writing a persuasive essay, do not give your readers any chance to critique your ideas, which means you have to make your logic as perfect as possible.

If you still do not know how to do it, you can find help through the following ways. First, ask an editor or a teacher to help you revise a single paragraph. The more you revise, the faster your writing improves. If you are currently in university, you can find help from the library. Every library has writing

help for free. Book an appointment now so you can learn the right techniques for academic writing. Second, simply pay attention to any academic writings published in books or journals. Study each paragraph and see how the linear logic unfolds and closes. In fact, if you have already read the majority part of this book, you will notice that the idea of each paragraph unfolds linearly. Third, you can go to *http://weibo.com/u/5056166870* and ask me questions. I welcome all kinds of questions concerning your writing and your studies.

Revision is magical, illuminating and effective. It is common sense that the "draft" should not be submitted to your teachers, yet many students still do it. A common mistake is to think that you can write a perfect paper the first time. The right way is to write an outline, then start a draft and revise it again and again. Revision not only betters your essay, but also makes you more intelligent because it gives you a chance to critique your own logic. During the revision process, you will discover your own logic flaws. By and by when you read other people's writings, you are able to identify logic flaws and raise critical questions. Any level 4 essay or "A" essay in university has been revised countless times. If in high school you develop a good habit of revising your own papers, you will

master longer essays in university.

The last step of revision is to "polish" your essay. After finishing your first draft, you revise your logic flow several times. When the argumentation is perfect, you now need to go back once again to check your grammatical errors, misspellings, punctuation errors, sentence structures and so forth. Most students, when first starting to learn how to edit their own papers, are most likely to take the "polish" process as the revision process. This will waste plenty of time. As you revise for the first or second time, you only need to pay attention to improving your content. The last round is to polish your language into perfect academic English.

Overcome Procrastination and Perfectionism

Procrastination is to delay what should be done. This is a common phenomenon. Everyone has procrastination issues, but what matters is how you deal with them. I used to know someone who could not hand in the paper even after being given an extension. This is a severe case. Mild procrastination is, say, you only start to do the homework one day before the deadline. You simply have to wait until the last minute. Underneath procrastination, there is always fear. Students all

understand the point of a deadline, but they fail to respect it because they are afraid that things cannot be done by then. A simple way to overcome procrastination is to give yourself an earlier deadline, and thus you do not have to be intimidated when the real deadline arrives. This is what I do with my studies. Whenever I had anxiety about a deadline, I created an earlier deadline so I could have things done two or three days ahead. Forget about the fear and plan ahead!

Procrastination usually goes hand in hand with perfectionism. The extreme perfectionist spends tons of time pondering the topic without actually writing a word. They want things to be so flawless that they end up writing nothing! Perfectionism blocks the mind, especially your logic flow. It is impossible for any logic to be flawless per se. Thus, there is no such thing as a "perfect essay"; you can even find flaws in professors' published articles. The nature of left-brain thinking is that the logic gap always exists no matter how careful you are. So, to overcome perfectionism, you need to get your outline and draft done without expecting them to be perfect. Just get started!

Training 3

Master English Pronunciation

How accurately you can pronounce English, if it is your second language, is a CHOICE. You can speak as accurately as any native English speakers. When I started learning my ABCs in middle school in China, my first teacher told me it was impossible for me to speak English like a native. At that time, I immediately realized it was because she could not speak like that! I believed I could speak English accurately if I wanted to.

Change Your Mindset

The key to achieve accurate English pronunciation, in my opinion, is not really the pronunciation training but a correct mindset. If you believe you can do it, you will naturally speak English well. The roadblock in many students' subconscious mind is, "I was not born here, so I can never speak like a

native. " This is not true; it is just your conscious choice. You can change the thought into something positive, say, "My English pronunciation is accurate, " and it will become accurate because you feel it is that way.

There is a kind of linguistic studies called " second language acquisition. " This kind of research is popular in China. For me, it is simple that you need to take your second language as if it is another "first language. " This means you learn as if you are a baby, which immediately switches your mindset so you can learn like a baby does. As a result, you can learn rapidly without that voice in your head—saying, "You are too old to learn a second language. " Actually, it is not the "second," but another "first. "

Having the right mindset means you have already done a great deal. The first tip is imitation. The right brain can acquire new things quickly. If you hear how a sound is pronounced, simply imitate it until you can pronounce it exactly the same way. The most useful way is to record your voice every day. When you replay your voice, flaws and inaccuracies can be easily identified. In this way, you can consciously correct your pronunciation. I had done this for a year until my pronunciation reached accuracy.

The second tip is to learn a little bit about phonetics.

Imitation is a quick way to pick up accurate pronunciation, but sometimes you still do not know how to pronounce sounds like "l," "th," "s," etc. This is why you need to know how you should position the tongue, teeth, palate, and so forth. You can require information from your ESL teachers or find books on phonetics from libraries to see the pictures that describe the production of every sound.

Since you are already here in an English-speaking country, your English pronunciation is supposed to improve quickly. If not, ask yourself if you are unconsciously avoiding speaking English or if you did not practice enough. Like I said before, you can absolutely be your own mentor and push yourself to success, or if you do not know the techniques, you can simply hire a coach to mentor you. English pronunciation is important but also a minor task. You should improve it within one or two months and let it go. By then you will have perfect pronunciation and will not have it as your roadblock.

Be 100% Confident

An accurate English pronunciation boosts your self-confidence in many ways. You may desire to learn new things well; you may want to make new friends; your personality may

change; you may want to shoulder more responsibilities. Problematic English pronunciation should not block you from larger successes. It does not have to be your story because now you know how to unlock your unlimited potential.

If you think you are a genius, you will be a genius. If you think you can achieve the impossible, you will achieve the impossible. If you think a certain difficulty is small, it will become small. If you think you can do something great, you can. You become your choice. The truth is that you deserve to have everything you want, and this is why you should be absolutely confident.

Training 4

University Application

During the process of university application, you will find that all the above theories and training will become extremely useful. This is the time to test whether you have found who you are, whether you have honed your craft, and whether you are qualified to enter a university. If you have done a good job laying a solid foundation for your academic studies, then the university application will become easy and exciting.

Make the University Want You

Being extremely competitive during the process of university applications is the key for you to excel. Thousands of students from all over the world are applying for the same program—why are you so different from others? You should spend time studying yourself rather than your competitors. Your unique voice distinguishes you from other applicants

because no one on earth has experienced your life. Your life shapes your passion, your dream, your genius, and your goals.

Usually, the must-have questions are who you think you are, why you are applying to the university, how you can contribute to the university's progress, and how you can serve humanity. If you have clear answers to these questions, then you can handle various questions the university may ask you. To make the university want you means you are rare; you know who you are and you can make a great contribution to the wellbeing of humanity. In this way, you can become the applicant who receives the offer earlier than others. In fact, a student I coached received her conditional admission two hours after submitting the online application.

The secret is that you are valuable enough. If the university does not give you an offer, it is their grave loss. Bear this in mind so you can get a bunch of offers and choose one from them.

When you compose the application document or prepare for an interview, your tone shows your confidence and your authenticity. First, by showing your confidence, you will appear certain about your goal. Some students' application papers sound like they are not sure whether they want to go to this university at all. The wishy-washy tone suggests that the applicants are not well-prepared. If you do not know what you

want, the university may not give you an offer. Your tone should sound determined, elegant, and indicate your familiarity with yourself and the university. Showing your confidence also suggests that your tone cannot sound like you are begging the university to have you.

Second, your tone shows that you are authentically you. Some students' application documents indicate "voices" from other places. Usually these students do not know how to write application essays, so they imitate other students' application papers. The voice thus is a hybrid; a focused central tone of the applicant is absent. This again shows that the applicant is not well prepared. Your chance of getting an offer is slim. Another case of lacking authenticity is that you pretend to be someone you are not. For example, you would like to study medicine, but your parents ask you to study finance. Your tone will reveal your insincerity because you cannot fake passion.

Why are you and the program (either an undergraduate or graduate program) a good match? This is the question you need to contemplate seriously. A thorough understanding of yourself allows you to know what on earth you can GIVE. Is your contribution to the world needed and appreciated by the university? If the university does not value you as an asset, it simply means you and the university are not a perfect match.

Feeling as though you are being valued also suggests that you might get scholarships. Because each program in North American is unique, your contribution to the program must somewhat propel the development of the said program. When you enter the right program, you will feel fulfilled, happy and productive.

A good match does not mean you have to CATER TO the needs of the university. In other words, you do not have to become someone you are not. This grave mistake lay in the fact that you will lose yourself. Even if you catered to every skill the program requires, chances are you might not get the offer whatsoever. If you can stay centered and bold enough to be who you really are, the right program will show up for you. This was what happened to me. I stayed true to my own passion because there was a deeper research question for me to solve. As a result, the right university gave me an offer and the right supervisor showed up. I was a bit intimidated in the beginning because he was such a big name in our field, but it was also a huge validation that my passion would guide me to the right people.

Focus on Your Mission and Legend

Many students, at the time they need to apply for a

university, never thought about why they needed to go to a university. Most of them think it is natural because their parents asked them to pursue higher education. It is natural to have a job after education and not before university education. Having a degree is also a huge brand builder. If you are not highly motivated, it is easy for you to give up when you face competition or a heavy workload.

I feel that the ultimate purpose in receiving higher education is to catapult you toward your personal mission and legend. Personal Legend—this concept—originally came from Paulo Coelho's *The Alchemist*. By personal legend I mean how you want to be recorded or remembered by history. Getting the university offer is just a start. To make the higher education meaningful, you need to constantly combine it with the questions we discussed in the "Self-Development" and "Self-Realization" sections. The exploration of these questions—who you are, how you can serve humanity, what is the value of your being, what legend you will leave for human history—will become your personal journey.

In the end, I wish you a happy and successful life.

THE END

Acknowledgements

Thank my parents for their everlasting support and love. I also want to thank all the students I have ever taught, especially Steven Zhang and Shu Lu. My sincere gratitude goes to Canadian writer Raymond Aaron, who inspired me to write this book. Thank Canadian gold medalist Mark McKoy for his kind support.